introduction

Every American city has its own personality: Chicago has Broad Shoulders, New York has the Great White Way. Cleveland certainly has its own personality too, but pinning us down to a word or a phrase is more difficult. Cleveland strives constantly to define and redefine its place in American culture.

When you come right down to it, our town is really nothing more than the sum total of the hopes, wants and dreams of its people. That's why this book is not about Cleveland, but rather the people who define it. They are a diverse group, as diverse as our town. Most you'll know right away, others you may be meeting for the first time. They include world-class athletes, entertainers, musicians and artists, and civic, business and religious leaders.

Many have helped shape our local and even national culture. Others work quietly behind the scenes to improve our daily lives. You may work with some of them, hear them on radio, or see them on TV. You may worship with them on Sunday, see them out and about on the town, or bump into them at the local grocery store.

Some grew up here, some traveled across the world to get here, others got their start here. But consider them all our neighbors. They all hold a special place in their heart for our city, their home.

These are their stories.

The Veteran Memorial Bridge

cleveland classics

great stories from the north coast

Photography by John Sobczak

Edited by Terry Troy

Foreword by Richard Osborne

Executive Editor: Richard Osborne

Copyeditor: Vivian Pospisil

Design: Jonathan Browning, Brown Ink Design

Library of Congress Cataloging-in-Publishing Data.
ISBN   0-9701-305-3-8   (soft cover edition)
ISBN   0-9701-305-2-x   (limited edition hard cover)

Produced by Lorien Studios

Printed by Friesens Corporation, Altona, Manitoba, Canada

The Center Street Bridge

The B&O Railroad Bridge #464

table of contents

fore

The Rapid Transit Authority Bridge

welcome to cleveland

The City of Cleveland has a history that is as rich and diverse as our many ethnic neighborhoods. From Tremont and Ohio City on our west side to Old Brooklyn south and Kinsman, Collinwood and Little Italy to the east, our neighborhoods combine to create a great city that is strong, vibrant and determined.

Every one of our neighborhoods has its own story, and every story has its own cast of characters. This book is about the extraordinary cast of characters who call Cleveland home. Their stories range from simple childhood recollections of the Cleveland that was to the wonder of seeing our City's skyline grow.

As you read these stories, you're certain to get an appreciation of what our City is all about. They should also spark a memory or two of your own: of riding the Flying Turns at Euclid Beach; taking the trolley from Ontario out to Cleveland Heights; seeing the Sterling Linder Christmas tree or Higbee's window during the holidays; or witnessing a favorite sports miracle.

These are stories of grit and determination, resiliency and sometimes regret, told by people who help define us as a City. I hope you enjoy them.

Jane L. Campbell
Mayor of Cleveland

cleveland classics

great stories from the north coast

bob Feller

t's true that I signed with the Cleveland Indians for one dollar and an autographed baseball back in 1935 when I was in high school, but that's just part of the story of how I got here. Times were certainly different back then. I grew up in Van Meter, Iowa, and that's where the Indians' Cy Slapnicka discovered me. Originally, I was supposed to go from Van Meter to Fargo where I'd play for $75 a month. During the Iowa State High School Baseball Tournament, I was doing all of the pitching, and my arm got so tight I couldn't pitch the last game. Well, I told the Cleveland ball club, and they told me to come to Cleveland and have one of their trainers look at my arm.

By the time I got here a few days later, my arm was in pretty good shape, so I went ahead and started pitching on the sandlots. They saw me pitching and decided to give me a chance pitching against the Cardinals in an exhibition game. It was the first week of July in 1936, the day before the All-Star game, which was in Boston that year. I struck out eight of nine in three innings. I joined the Indians in Philadelphia the Thursday after the All-Star game, so I never went to Fargo and I never played minor league ball.

The rule in those days was that all minor league clubs had territorial rights to sign the players from a specific region. The Des Moines Club claimed that I should have signed with them, but my dad refused to let me sign with them. I suppose they could have sold me to a big league club and gotten some sort of compensation, so they complained to the league. I told Kenesaw Mountain Landis, who was the commissioner of baseball, that I thought I was treated fairly by the Indians, so he fined the Indians $7,500 and let me stay here. That rule was soon changed and many players got their free agency a couple of years later.

When I first came to Cleveland what I noticed most was the noise and confusion of a major city, which really didn't bother me all that much — especially when I got my uniform on and was on the mound. I stayed at a rooming house at 1910 East 89th Street, which of course has long since been demolished. I remember there was a Civil War veteran who stayed there. He joined the Union Army when he was 16 years old, so we sat on the porch every night and I would listen to him tell Civil War stories. It was right near the old Bolton Hotel, which is where I moved the following year

Back then, we played weekend games at Cleveland Municipal Stadium and the rest at League Park. I liked League Park. It was 375 feet down the left field line and about 460 feet to center. The power alleys were about 415. The right field line was only about 290 feet, but it also had a screen about 50 feet high. Left-handed hitters loved the park because of that shortened porch.

It only seated about 24,000 and it was very difficult to find a place to park. People came to the game mostly by streetcars and buses. The fans loved League Park because they were so close to the players.

That first year I tied the Major League record with 17 strikeouts in a game. It was against the Philadelphia Athletics and they had a lot of hard-swinging, right-handed hitters — which I had better luck with most of the time. I can't really remember what kind of a day it was. When I was on the mound, it was just the batter and me. I kind of tuned everything else out. Of course, with my backup, the defensive players, I really didn't have too much to worry about.

I was throwing my high fastball a lot, which was going right by Philadelphia's right handers. They had a couple of left handers, like Wally Moses, who was hard to strike out, but for the most part I was going against right handers. For some reason, I was behind the count with the hitters quite often that day. I had better control on my curve than my fastball, so when I was behind in the count, I would throw my curve. A lot of pitchers like to throw their fastball at three and two, but I always liked my curve. Of course, during my career I didn't hit the plate every time, and there were a few people who hit home runs off the curve, but that day I got a lot of called third strikes.

When World War II came, like most other young men I enlisted. I was on my way to Cleveland to renegotiate my contract when I heard about Pearl Harbor. So instead of coming to Cleveland, I went straight to Chicago and enlisted at the Navy recruiting office. I took training at the Norfolk War College and then served on the U.S.S. Alabama. I came home in 1945 and went on inactive duty after coming back from the Pacific.

We left League Park for good in 1946 and started playing all of our games at Municipal Stadium. I liked that park too. That was under Bill Veeck. Of course, one of my best baseball memories was the Championship season of 1948. I think we had a better team in 1948 than we did in 1954 when we won 111 and blew the Series in four straight. We had very good pitching in 1954, but we got in a batting slump. I retired in 1956, but was still very active with the club for years afterward.

Obviously, Cleveland and the Cleveland Indians played a very big

> **It's true that I signed with the Cleveland Indians for one dollar and an autographed baseball back in 1935 when I was in high school, but that's just part of the story of how I got here.**

part in my life, but it's not the only reason I made Cleveland home. I think it has more to do with the people in this city. My fondest memories are when Cy Slapnicka and his wife were here. We were very well received, and made quite a few friends — and that's really why I stayed here. After baseball, I was in the hotel business with both Hilton and Sheraton, and then I was in the insurance business for 16 years. I met quite a few people going to various business functions and civic affairs. I still like to go to ballgames, and now and then I'll still go to training camp to sign autographs.

Of course, the old family farm in Iowa is long gone. I sold it back in 1957. There's really not too much left for me in Iowa. Throughout the years I've made many wonderful friends in Cleveland, and my wife Anne likes it here as well. I guess the real reason we are still here is because of the special relationships we've developed with the people who call Cleveland home. ☙

*Bob Feller, pitching legend and member
of the Baseball Hall of Fame.
Photographed at his home in Gates Mills.*

john Lanigan

I heard a lot about Cleveland before I ever came here. I was just this kid from Nebraska in Denver working for Joe Finan. He told me all the stories about Cleveland — how Rock and Roll started here and about all the music that came out of this town. It made it seem like such an exciting place to work. I remember working at a station in Albuquerque in the mornings when someone said, "They have a new morning man over at KOB across the street — and he's coming in from Cleveland." I thought I was doomed, they have somebody from Cleveland coming in, I won't survive. That was the image of it all.

So when I got a call from Jack Thayer at WGAR while I was in Dallas, it was the thought of the job that was more intriguing than the city itself. I would be coming in to replace Imus, who was heading off to New York. I flew in in the middle of winter, so I really didn't get a good first impression of the town. But I knew I was going to be a part of a scene I had heard quite a bit about. And Cleveland turned out to be a great town for me.

I got here and started out on WGAR and we had a lot of fun. Two years later, I was doing something called the "Prize Movie" on WUAB TV43.

When I first came here I moved into a brand-new condominium development called Ledgewood out in Strongsville. I used to ride my bike around the development quite a bit. One day, I ran into Jack Moffet, the station manager of Channel 43, and we ended up riding around together. He said he was looking for somebody for the "Prize Movie" because the guy who was going to do it had started radio in the afternoon.

"If you're looking for somebody, I could probably do it," I told him.

"But you're replacing Imus, you're a little too risqué for this kind of thing," he said.

So we just rode together and talked. The next day he asked if I could come in and cut an audition tape. The day after that, he asked if I could start Monday.

We actually went in and cut an audition tape, and there were all kinds of people there — including this one lady who wanted to host the show with her dog.

So there was an interesting cross-section of people at the audition. At any rate, that's how I got the job — but it wasn't very big pay. The first few years we got $25 a show — it was really just something to keep me busy in the afternoon.

But it did spread my name around the market — and even into a four-state area where the "Prize Movie" was shown. I did it for almost 20 years, so I really got associated with it. I used to go on vacations and people would recognize me, "Hey you're that Prize Movie guy!" they'd shout. It's nice to have that kind of recognition.

Obviously, the focus of my career has been radio. We've had a lot of fun over the years, doing our skits. And some of the things we did off the air! Dog-sled races through the town. Jumping out of airplanes. Flying with both the Blue Angels and the Thunderbirds. Then, of course, there were the things we did on the air, like the funny phone calls — of course you can't do that anymore, but we always tried to do it in fairly good taste.

More satisfying though, were the thousands of interviews. I have a couple of favorites. The most fun was Alan Bean, the astronaut. He had some great stories about being on the Apollo Mission. He told everyone how, when he got to the dark side of the moon and was out of range for Houston, he'd take the controls of the capsule and play around just to see what it could do. He told us how the astronauts went to the bathroom and how urine was ejected from the capsule.

I guess once they ejected urine into space, it turned into thousands of glistening little stars. Everyone on board ran to the window to look out the capsule and watch this glistening little meteor shower from the urine. He had a lot of neat little stories like that. He was certainly one of my favorite interviews.

I also liked the time I interviewed Jimmy Carter, but more because the interview was so touching. He was no longer president and had just come out with a book of poetry. I wanted him to read a poem about putting his dog to sleep. He said it would be a tough one to do, but said he'd do it anyway. As he started to read this very touching poem about having to take out his dog and shoot it back in the old days on his ranch, I actually could see him start to break down. He had a real hard time, but he finished it. It was very moving, actually sublime.

The people I've met here have been fantastic as well. One of my biggest thrills was meeting Bill Randle. When I first came to Cleveland, Bill Randle asked if I'd speak at Kent State. I really didn't want to but he said, "Come on, I'll pick you up and fly you in my plane down to Kent State." So I went.

As someone who grew up in the business, Bill Randle was, of course, a very big name. When he was inducted to the Cleveland Area Broadcasters Hall of Fame, he actually called and asked if I'd introduce him at the ceremony. It was a thrill. Bill Randle was much more than a radio personality. He was brilliant. He was an attorney and an educator. He was a lot of things. He was the kind of person who made the industry better, just by being in it. Getting to know him and having him respect me was a highlight of my career.

> **When I first came to Cleveland, Bill Randle asked if I'd speak at Kent State. I really didn't want to but he said, "Come on, I'll pick you up and fly you in my plane down to Kent State." So I went.**

Cleveland has been a great town for me. I love the people. They're all nice. I also love that Cleveland is a very easy town to live in. You don't have the same traffic nightmares as other cities such as New York, Los Angeles, Chicago or Boston. But it has its other side too. A side that wants to maintain the status quo. It's almost as if there is an element of the "old guard" that doesn't embrace people coming in from outside the town and being successful. I think it's hurt the city somewhat.

But like I said, Cleveland's been a great town for me.

John Lanigan, host of the
"Lanigan and Malone Show," WMJI.
Photographed at Edgewater Park, Cleveland.

sam Rutigliano

to this day, people always ask me about Red Right 88. I never get into the reasons why I made the call because people will never really understand all the things we do as coaches. But that play marked the end of a very exciting two weeks that changed my life forever.

There was a chemistry and magic about the City of Cleveland that I never imagined possible. I never thought that a football team could light up an entire town. To this day, people still talk about the reign of the Kardiac Kids, comparing it to those of Paul Brown and Blanton Collier—but people always say that our era was the most exciting — and that's the real magic of it.

Even though I left the Browns and went to coach at Liberty University, and then went to Europe for four years with NFL Europe, I always maintained my residence here. I knew that this city was the best thing for my family, my three kids. One still lives here and teaches at Mayfield. One lives in Virginia and another lives in Dallas, but they all view Cleveland as their hometown.

Being a football coach was a lifelong dream. I grew up in a section of Brooklyn called Sheepshead Bay in the same neighborhood as Joe Paterno and Vince Lombardi. Obviously, I never climbed the mountains they climbed, but it was something I emulated from the very beginning.

My mom was born in New York City, but my dad was born in Italy and immigrated here. He was a truck driver for a bakery company; my mom worked at the same company and that's how they met. He always knew that the real passport to this country was to get an education. I played high school football at Erasmus Hall in New York, and got a scholarship to the University of Tennessee. When the recruiter came to my house, my father just couldn't understand how they would give you the opportunity to get an education, along with room, board, books and tuition, just for playing football.

When I graduated I came back to New York City and took a job at Lafayette High School and coached there for three years while getting my master's in education from Columbia University. From there I went to Greenwich High School in Connecticut and then to Chappaqua in Westchester County, New York. For eight years I was a high school coach, but the dream of being a college coach was always there.

I finally got my chance at the University of Connecticut. As a matter of fact, Lou Holtz and I started together at the University of Connecticut. I left there for the University of Maryland where I was the assistant coach under Lou Saban — who, incidentally, played for the Browns. The last game of the 1966 season, he told me in strictest confidence that he was going to the Denver Broncos. I was a little hesitant, but I followed him there. The opportunity was just too big. Only three years before I was a high school coach. Now, I was going to the pros.

From the time I started coaching until the time I joined Cleveland, our family moved 19 times. My children attended 23 schools. In Cleveland there was a gentleman by the name of Peter Hadhazy and, of course, Art Modell. They were the two who really gave me the opportunity to fulfill my dream of becoming a head coach.

When I was named head coach of the Browns in 1978, Pittsburgh had won the World Championship that same year. They would repeat the next year. Houston was in the AFC Championship Game those same two years. Cincinnati would make a showing in the Super Bowl in 1981. So the AFC Central was the toughest division in pro football.

When I got the job, I called every player on the Browns roster and told them that I had gotten the job, and what I expected of each one of them. I told them that I didn't expect to have any credibility until I proved it. Being the head coach, I told them they would have to earn their credibility with me as well.

When I got to Brian Sipe, he said to me: "Get me a quarterback coach with a system and surround me with smart people. Then get five condominiums up in front of me to protect me, because my arm is sufficient. I can win." Instinctively, I knew something was there. I asked the owner and general manager what they thought of Sipe, and they said he couldn't play — that we would not win with him. I decided I wouldn't listen to them. I learned a lot about coaching by learning what not to do.

So I talked to the guys on television, people like Len Dawson, Fran Tarkenton and Bob Griese — guys who were successful quarterbacks, but who didn't really fit the prototype of an NFL quarterback. "What do you think of Sipe?" I'd ask. And each one said the same thing: "He throws strikes. He hits open targets and he has a great presence." But a quarterback is like a tea bag, you don't know what you got until you get him in hot water. When I put Sipe in hot water, he performed — and that was good enough for me.

But a quarterback is like a tea bag, you don't know what you got until you get him in hot water. When I put Sipe in hot water, he performed — and that was good enough for me.

Three years later, he was the MVP of the National Football League. He eclipsed every record of every quarterback that had ever played for the Browns — and starting with Otto Graham, there were a lot of good ones. He was the guy who led us to the championship of the AFC Central, which was then the NFL's toughest.

I remember flying back from Cincinnati after we had clinched the division. We couldn't get into the jetway at the airport — there were too many people. So we taxied to what was then the old tank plant. They had a stairway, and a big platform. When I stepped off the plane, I saw Mayor Voinovich was there to greet us — along with thousands of people.

As I said before, it was the beginning of a magical two weeks. I couldn't even go to the post office without someone coming up to me. It was just glorious. I remember driving along the freeway and there was this big sign that said "God Bless Sam Rutigliano." And I said to myself, "That's really heavy." But it was also unbelievable for my wife and family.

Sam Rutigliano, football coach.
Photographed at George Finnie Stadium,
Baldwin-Wallace College.

I still hear about that play — Red Right 88 — even to this very day.

I was coaching at Liberty University and we were playing at Eastern Michigan. We were undefeated. It was 1989. So I'm sitting on the sidelines and I notice this big sign, as big as a wall. And it says, "Red Right 88." And I'm thinking to myself, "There has to be some wacko from Cleveland here, because only he and I can share this—no one else really gives a damn."

So I still have moments like that. I was in New Zealand once with a Division III football team and we were playing an exhibition game. A writer came up and asked me about Red Right 88. So it went from Cleveland, to eastern Michigan, all the way to New Zealand.

I was at a tribute dinner once and Brian Sipe got up to speak. He is a perceptive, bright guy. So he gets up, looks at me and says, "We did what we did all year — what we did all those years as the Kardiac Kids. We were on fire and we were doing what we did best. The thing I hold on to after all of these years is that you trusted me. That you put it in my hands."

And it was true. I knew it the minute I was swarmed by reporters after that game on that frozen field so many years ago. When they all came up to me and asked about my decision to go with Sipe rather than kick the field goal. And I gave them the same answer I still give to everyone today: "My mother always told me that the girl you take to the dance is the one you bring home. Brian Sipe got us here. He was our best opportunity to win."

When they all came up to me and asked about my decision to go with Sipe rather than kick the field goal. And I gave them the same answer I still give to everyone today: "My mother always told me that the girl you take to the dance is the one you bring home.
Brian Sipe got us here. He was our best opportunity to win."

To this day, people always ask me about Red Right 88. I never get into the reasons why I made the call because people will never really understand all the things we do as coaches. But that play marked the end of a very exciting two weeks that changed my life forever.

molly Shannon

for me, Cleveland is all about close friends and family. I left Cleveland to go to college in New York in 1983, but I still think of it as home. I have so many amazing memories of growing up there.

I grew up in Shaker Heights on Winchell Road and my best friend Anne Pountney lived a block away. We were always together. When we were little she would meet me half way to her house and we'd find something to do for the day. When we got older we would go down to Tommy's on Coventry. I used to work there as a busboy. It was just a summer job, but a lot of fun. Tommy was such a nice guy and I liked the food there. So Tommy's is a very Cleveland thing for me. When I'm back in town, I still go there.

Anne's parents and my dad were really good friends too. They used to have parties where they would drink and get really crazy. A lot of characters I do are composites of people I saw at those parties. But I would never do an impression of anyone directly because I would never want to hurt anyone's feelings. They're just bits and pieces of the many characters Anne and I saw at those parties.

My fondest memories are of hanging out at Van Aken, going to Cafe Adagio to get coffee with my dad. Or going to the drugstore or Noggin's. I lost my mother when I was young so my dad and I were very close.

He would pick me up from school with some lame excuse, and I would actually cut school with him. We'd drive over to Edgewater Park and make a day of it. Swinging on those terrific swings they have there. Just hanging out, talking about life with my dad. Talking and laughing.

He would always take me to old movies. And because he was so into it, I naturally became into it — not that I was trying to please him — it just seemed so natural.

I went to St. Dominic's and that's where I got interested in performing. I would dance during St. Patrick's Day Shows. The teachers would bring all the classes together and each class would pick a song and we'd dance to it. Not the fancy River Dance thing, just basic Irish Jigs — but I lived for it every year.

Later I got into Heights Youth Theatre. It was a performing company run by Jerry Leonard and we put on very elaborate plays in Cleveland Heights. Productions like the "Wizard of Oz," "Oliver" and "Alice in Wonderland." It was very professional children's theater and pretty intense. It was the greatest training ever. I'm still friends with Jerry's daughter Wendy who lives in New York.

Breaking into show business was tough. I did a Hertz commercial, then I was on "Twin Peaks." I got some small parts on soap operas, and did Denny's breakfast buffet commercials, but I was still working as a hostess in a restaurant.

Through it all, my dad was very encouraging.

I started making enough money doing commercials, so I quite my job at the restaurant. Soon afterward I got my big break on SNL. Everybody back home who knew me was so excited, and so encouraging — all the people I went to grade school and high school with — I'm still good friends with many of them. I just can't begin to tell you what that meant to me.

My fondest memories are of hanging out at Van Aken, going to Cafe Adagio to get coffee with my dad. Or going to the drugstore or Noggin's. I lost my mother when I was young so my dad and I were very close.

Those are my memories of home. There are a lot of people in show business from Cleveland and whenever we get together, we talk about what an amazing place it truly is. I love Cleveland and I could live there. But in show business you have to live in New York or LA.

I still have relatives and friends there so I'm back all the time. I love driving around the highways, going to Corky and Lenny's and driving around the Heights.

It's a little different going back there, now that my dad has passed away. I miss him, of course.

But it still feels great going back. It's just different knowing he's not there.

We'd drive over to Edgewater Park and make a day of it. Just hanging out, talking about life with my dad.

Molly Shannon, comedian and actress.
Photographed at her home in Manhattan.

had a great nine years as a member of the Cleveland Browns and a member of the community. I knew I had a great relationship with the fans when I played. I didn't understand how exceptional that relationship was until I came through promoting my book, *Out of Bounds.*

I really had a chance to meet the fans one-on-one, and it was only then that I began to understand what we shared. They would tell me stories of how they went to see a game when they were young with their father. Sometimes a son would go with a father, or a whole family would go. In some cases, the father had passed away, and the son was now all grown up. They identified so strongly with being together at the game, and they identified me as the star player. So it was a genuine connection that we had, but I never really knew that until I did my book tour. It was a truly great experience because many times, as a player, you don't know how genuine the fans are.

The Cleveland fans have been very forgiving and loving in their relationship with me over the years — and I'm very happy to be able to say that.

I'm also happy that I had such a close relationship with the African American community while I was in Cleveland. A lot of times, especially today, black stars don't hang out in the black and poor communities. They're aloof. But I think it's really important. It was something I learned from Muhammad Ali.

When he refused induction into military service, we had a summit of black athletes in Cleveland. Back then, I had an economic development organization, the Negro Industrial and Economic Union, and we all met in my office. We had Kareem Abdul Jabaar, Freddie McClinton from Kansas City, Bill Russell from the Celtics, Bobbie Mitchell from the Browns — we even had Mayor Carl Stokes. This was a very educated and very socially conscious group of individuals — people who were well versed in history.

When the meeting was over Muhammad looks at me and says, "Let's take a walk." I asked, "Walk? Where we going to walk to?" And he said, "Let's just go out and walk and talk to the people."

So we went out to the barbershops and hairdressers in the neighborhood. We stopped at the grocery stores. And the people were so happy just to see us together. At the time, Muhammad was really popular, and a big part of his life was walking into the black and poor communities. It was an attitude that really defined a lot of the black athletes of the day. Today, there isn't that same kind of consciousness. But there is a need among young black kids today, to see their heroes.

Obviously, I had many memorable moments on the playing field. When I came to Cleveland in the late '50s, I knew Paul Brown was looking for a running back. When I scored a touchdown in my first exhibition game, Paul pulled me out of the game and said, "You're my new fullback," and those were the greatest words I ever heard.

We played for the championship three times, and won it once in 1964, shutting out the great Baltimore Colts. It was a real team effort. Gary Collins was MVP, Frank Ryan had a great game. I had a decent game. Everybody praised the offense after the game, but what they didn't realize was how great our defense was. They shut out the Baltimore Colts. The defense was simply unbelievable, but a lot of people don't realize that.

Still, Cleveland fans are the best. I hope they can find a way to forgive Art Modell. He really didn't have a choice. He got himself into a bad financial situation, and moving the team was the only way out. He did allow us to keep the name and colors, and that's important.

When I came to Cleveland in the late '50s, I knew Paul Brown was looking for a running back. When I scored a touchdown in my first exhibition game, Paul pulled me out of the game and said, "You're my new fullback," and those were the greatest words I ever heard.

The one positive that came out of that was that I got to meet Al Lerner. He was one of the most powerful and rich but unassuming and likable men that I have ever met. And we became good friends. During the season, I would call him every Monday and discuss the game. His death shocked me. I miss him.

Now Randy is in charge of the team, and I'm sure he'll do a good job. In three or four years, the Browns will once again be a powerful, successful franchise. They are the new Browns — I was a part of the old Browns. But I'm sure Randy will keep the Browns legacy alive.

The Cleveland fans have been very forgiving and loving in their relationship with me over the years

Jim Brown, football Hall of Famer, actor and activist.
Photographed at his home overlooking the city of Los Angeles.

dick Goddard

When you're a weather forecaster, you're always going to irritate someone, no matter how good your forecast is. There is just so much real estate to cover here in Northeast Ohio that you're going to be wrong somewhere. Considering that, it amazes me that I've been able to hang on as long as I have. I've been on television now for more than 43 years. The funny part is, I only went on television so I could have a story to tell my grandchildren one day. I really wanted to be an artist with Walt Disney.

I grew up just south of Akron, actually north of Massillon, in a town called Greensburg, which is now just called Green. I started in weather forecasting when I joined the Air Force in 1951. It was during the Korean War, but the government in all of their wisdom assigned me to the 6th Weather Squadron out of Tinker Air base in Oklahoma. It was quite an experience. I got to fly around a lot and even witnessed the first H-Bomb test over the Bikini Islands in the South Pacific — that was incredible.

After I got out of the service, I started working with the Weather Bureau at the Akron-Canton Airport, but I was also going to Kent State. I eventually graduated with a Bachelor of Fine Arts. I sent my portfolio to Disney Studios. They said they would love to talk to me and for me to come on out.

At the Akron-Canton Airport's Weather Bureau I was doing some radio broadcasts. The general manager of KYW-TV in Cleveland called and asked if I'd like to be on TV, but I refused. "I can't do that," I told him. "I had only one speech class at Kent and I'm petrified of going on television."

But after I said "no," he called again, and the guys at the bureau wouldn't leave me alone. "Why not try it?" they said. "Then you can at least tell your grandchildren that you were once on TV."

So I decided to try it once and that would be it — then I'd head out to Disney. Forty-three years later, I'm still on TV. I still have that letter from Disney. One of these days, I'm going to call them and see if the offer still stands.

But seriously, I don't think people on television today realize the power we have as weather forecasters. I hear disc jockeys talking about the weather all the time, how it's going to rain this weekend or on this day, or that it will snow next week. I don't think they really understand the effect we can have on the local economy. It's a very big responsibility and one I take very seriously.

In fact, there was only one time that I remember that I actually went on the air and told people they had better stay home the next day.

It was in January of 1978. The storm came out of the Gulf of Mexico, a delta low barreling straight at us, gathering isobars as it came. I remember going on the air and saying, "Folks, this is one monster. Don't plan on going anywhere tomorrow."

I lived out in Lakewood back then. I waited until four in the morning, and nothing happened. I said, "My God, I'm out of work — I've just blown it." All of a sudden, the thing hit and it was incredible. On January 26, 1978, the barometer hit 28.28, the lowest pressure ever recorded in the State of Ohio. The winds were clocked at up to 110 miles per hour. I came to work that morning and the snow was horizontal. When it hit your exposed flesh, it was like acupuncture. I called it the White Hurricane. It was the most violent winter storm we ever had in this area, and we nailed it.

I have many fond memories of Cleveland and Northeast Ohio. I'm a big sports nut. In fact, I've been doing the Browns stats for radio for more than 33 years now.

I'm very happy that we have been able to grow the Woollybear Festival into what it is today. I came up with the idea in 1973, and we only had about 400 people at the first one. It was just a small parade in Birmingham, which is where it all started. Now it's in Vermilion, and we get over 100,000 people. One time we had a three-hour parade with up to 32 high school bands marching. So it's really grown. It's a great

> **It was in January of 1978. The storm came out of the Gulf of Mexico, a delta low barreling straight at us, gathering isobars as it came. I remember going on the air and saying, "Folks, this is one monster. Don't plan on going anywhere tomorrow."**

festival and it's great for the kids. It's something I'm very proud of.

I am also very proud of the fact that I have been able to help animals. The station allows me on Thursday to show animals that people bring in. We try to help find them a home, and then on Friday we head out to the Cuyahoga County kennel and show some of the animals there. I guess my love for animals all goes back to my days growing up on the farm down in Greensburg. My grandpa used to tell me, "As you go through life, it isn't the quadrupeds you have to worry about, it's the carbon-based bipeds—the two footed animals." Boy was he right.

Most of the people here have been very good to me. You get some people who are screwballs and others who are the highest squirrel in the tree, but that's the trade-off. I am just very happy that I can do what I am doing. And I am humbled by the fact I have been able to last this long in really a tough business. ✏

Dick Goddard, meteorologist.
Photographed on the set of FOX 8 News.

sam Miller

most people know me as a businessman, civic leader and a developer, but what they don't know is that I grew up poor on Cleveland's near east side, just off 63rd and Woodland.

It was tough growing up there. You fought your way to school and you fought your way back home at night. I went to Woolridge Elementary School, which is no longer in existence. My parents didn't speak much English, but they were hardworking and smart.

I grew up in a Jewish household and I am still, to this day, very proud to be a religious Jew. I was seven years old, and I had just learned how to read and write. It was winter and I wanted a sled more than anything else — but my parents couldn't afford a sled. Every time I'd ask, they'd say, "Not now."

Back then, the *Cleveland News* had a sports editor named Ed Bang, who ran a Christmas Club. So I decided to write a letter to Ed Bang. The deal was, if he liked your letter, you would get what Santa Claus was supposed to bring you for Christmas. So I sent off my letter and a few days later there was a knock on the door. They asked, "Do you have a Sam Miller living here?" And my mother said, "Yes, he's my son." They told her they had a Christmas present for her son, Sam. And my mother said, "We don't believe in Christmas." She turned him down. I couldn't have it.

Many people try to hide the fact that they are Jewish, but I am proud of it. For 6,000 years we have been hearing that we are a dying people. As long as we keep hearing that, we are still around.

Growing up in Cleveland wasn't all bad. I did get a few breaks for which I'm grateful. My mother scrimped and saved pennies so I could go to college. Back then, tuition at Western Reserve University was about $300 a year, so I went there. At the end of three years I had earned some scholastic and athletic achievements. There was a dean at Western Reserve who took a liking to me, Dean Huntley, who encouraged me to apply to Harvard because they were giving out scholarships. I told him I didn't think they would accept me, and they probably didn't take people from my class. But he kept encouraging me, so I finally applied and got in.

My mother, God bless her memory, said, "If you are going to Harvard, I'm going to make sure you have a suitcase for your clothes." So she found a suitcase without any handles. Before I left, she fashioned handles out of laundry rope. I thought this was par for the course. When I got to Harvard, I was one of the last to walk into the dormitory. I took one look at all the other suitcases, and was ashamed. I should have been proud, but I was ashamed. I didn't know what to do, so I hid my suitcase and unpacked when no one was looking.

I have been very successful. I have been involved with numerous real estate developments in Cleveland, but I'm more proud of what I have been able to accomplish as a philanthropist.

So she found a suitcase without any handles. Before I left, she fashioned handles out of laundry rope. I thought this was par for the course. When I got to Harvard, I was one of the last to walk into the dormitory. I took one look at all the other suitcases, and was ashamed. I should have been proud, but I was ashamed.

Yet despite my professional success, when people ask me where I learned the most in life, I usually say, "Gutter University." It's the most valuable education you can get, because it gives you a radar. When you see somebody, two antennae go up and in seven seconds you can tell whether you have a phony or not. It's been very valuable to me throughout my career because when you find someone who's genuine you can be very loyal.

And I'm very loyal to the people in my life.

...when people ask me where I learned the

Sam Miller, Co-Chairman and Treasurer, Forest City Enterprises.
Photographed in his Tower City office.

host in life, I usually say, "Gutter University."

helga Sandburg

Remembering is a dream that comes in waves.

Dear love, I said to you from in the dream,
Say what makes the willow tree so green,
Say what makes the light on the pale skin gleam,
Say while we lie together in the dream.

Your mouth on mine I heard your heart repeat,
The willow's roots are long and dark and sweet,
The pale light is the space where voices meet.
Then where is love? I heard my quick heart beat.

Love, you said, is of its own self wove,
It is not us, there is no act to prove.
In its green time this thing will choose to move,
And then into the dream stood love.

It was fall of 1963. I wrote that poem to Barney when I made up my mind to marry him. He sent a letter to my father, "Dear Mr. Sandburg, I am Helga's Barney — Dr. George Crile, Jr., head of the department of General Surgery at the Cleveland Clinic. I am the one who wants to marry your daughter. To be more precise I am the one whom she is thinking of marrying."

I feel what my mother says, "Finally, a doctor!" I'd been married to a herdsman and a professor and had left them. Barney wants to ask Carl's permission, so we visit Connemara Farm in North Carolina. Carl marries us. "Swipes, do you want to marry this man?" "Yes, sire!" "Then do you take him for your lawful wedded husband?" "I do." "And do you, Barney Crile...?" And he does.

I met Barney when I lived in Washington through Kay Halle, a friend of mine. She wanted me to come to a party as his date. He'd been devastated by the loss of his his wife, who was Kay's sister. All I could foresee was this ancient bearded man who wanted to talk about his dead wife. I could handle it. But then I got other invitations. I tried to back out, but Kay held me to my promise.

So I met Barney. Stunningly handsome. Graying hair and wild blue eyes.

"Hi. I'm Helga" "I understand you write poetry." But it's the way he says it, acerbic. "That's right and I get along just fine." I start talking to other people.

Then we were interested in one another. It was love. I was born in November of 1918 and he was 11 years older — in November of 1907. It worked.

So I came to Cleveland in 1963. Just after Kennedy's assassination. It was a bittersweet ending to my Washington days, holding fast to Barney's enormous love.

I liked the house and the animals in the yard. But there were some feelings in his family. "You're in the catbird seat." That sort of thing. "What do you want me to do?"

"Here's the reality of it," Barney says.

He and I shared the same principles. He was interested in what I did as a writer. He writes, but doesn't know how fiction writers write. "It's the same thing," I say. "You have ideas and you just put them down."

We had written unicorn poems to each other after meeting. We built a place out in the country called the Unicorn's Lair.

Soon I'm taking care of the bills, doing the management. It's a true partnership. Barney loves it. He has no interest in money. Not much interest in going places around town either. "Do we have to go to the symphony?" he asks. "Sweetie, we don't have to go anywhere you don't want to go." When I first arrive, he takes me to the Cleveland Play House. We're right up front. I'm in heaven. But then I hear "schnnoooorrrksk." He's totally gone, absolutely out of it.

So I go with friends. He's happy that I enjoy myself.

Then, 25 years later, "I'm going down to my office at the Clinic," he says. He seldom goes to his office. Something's going on. But I would never ask him why. If there's something he wants to tell me he'll tell me.

After a while he came back and told me. It was in his lungs. You don't go into panic. You don't go into histrionics — that's not something you do with someone you know. I had had cancers before. I even wrote a poem called "On Learning I May Be About to Die."

"How long do you have?" I ask.

"Who knows," he says.

One of the high points of Barney's life was getting his autobiography, "The Way It Was — Sex, Surgery, Treasure and Travel — 1907 to 1987," published. He sat in his chair in the living room and wrote it. His mother had saved everything he ever wrote, thought or did. And the Cleveland Clinic had all of their archives.

The book was out while he was still alive — which for me was heavenly — because it was heaven for him. After he died, they had a party at Booksellers and everyone came. He wasn't there, but his spirit was. It was wonderful.

I like being single again. At 85, the family worries. The stairways in this big house look dangerous. But I go up and down these steps three times a day, with the wash, books, manuscripts, bird feed — whatever. I am not lonely. Loneliness is when you really need somebody. Solitude is chosen. There is a holiness to it. I once wrote a poem on the subject

Am I waiting for a knock upon the door?
Is it death or the next day or a friend or child I'm waiting for?
And when I hear it will I rise and lift the latch
And find no one? Will my caller be loneliness come to watch
Me stalk about my rooms? I'll draw a chair
And make him welcome saying, Oh where
Have you been? Are you afraid? You must not hide
And come more often, please. Don't remain outside
Wandering up and down the stair. I hear you sometimes in the night
And it disturbs my rest. I've often wanted to invite
You in. Do you ever stand in the shadow at the bookcase?
Am I wrong in mentioning that I've seen your face
Now that we are at last eye to eye? Have you been lost
In my mirror's dark?Now that I have found you, stay dear guest.

People ask me when I'll leave my house. That will be when they take me out feet first. Until then, I have my garden and the Unicorn's Lair and my library and my friends and family. In my books and lectures, I have said everything I wanted to say.

Helga Sandburg Crile, writer, novelist and poet.
Photographed at her home in Cleveland Heights.

viktor Schreckengost

all good design starts with function. I'll give you a good example. Look at the chair I'm sitting in. You know how it was designed?

I made up a barrel with a device on top that had soft clay covered with plastic. I sat outside the Murray Ohio cafeteria and offered a chit for a free cup of coffee for anyone who would sit on my chair. After I got about 300 fanny impressions, I took the top off and made a cast right from it. It's made from one piece of stamping and one piece of tubing, but it's still very comfortable.

So that's design, and that's what much of my career has been about. But I guess I'm still a kid at heart. Looking back on my career as an artist, designer and teacher, I got the most fun out of designing toys — the bicycles and pedal cars.

I always knew the children would love them. I didn't know about their parents, but as long as the children loved them, I knew they would be popular.

I started designing toys when I was five or six years old. We made our own, we didn't have any. My dad would help us make everything. He'd give us the stuff to work with and then he'd help us assemble them — all kinds of wagons, push devices. Some of them translated into the designs you see today.

Of course, we also made pottery and dishes. I grew up in Sebring, Ohio, which was the pottery town. My father moved there to help open French China production. So I grew up there, in the potteries. That's how I got interested in art and design. I made dishes at a very young age, too. My father would take them in, and fire and glaze them. That was just so much fun.

I came here in 1925 to attend what was then the Cleveland School of Art. It's now the Cleveland Institute of Art. After I graduated, I taught there for many years and headed up their design department. That's been the most rewarding aspect of my career, passing on the fundamentals of good design to so many who are now at the top of their fields. It's also very rewarding to have my work displayed in so many museums around the world. But like I said, I had the most fun with the toys.

Actually, my work designing sets for the theater actually led to my work with Murray Ohio and their bicycles. I was designing stages for my friend Barclay Leathem, who was putting on plays to raise money to refurbish a tavern. This was back in 1938. So I went over to Barclay's apartment to show him some sketches for some sets, and we were joined by his friend and upstairs neighbor Ralph O'Brien, who was a vice president at Murray.

O'Brien's wife made some drinks, and before we knew it, we had polished off a whole bottle of whiskey. That's when we started talking about bicycles. Murray had been getting their designs from an artist who was big on design but not on engineering. A lot of his designs couldn't be made into anything practical.

So O'Brien asked me if I'd like to design a bike, and I said sure. He told me to come down to Murray the next Monday and we'd get started. Only I didn't know whether I should keep the meeting or not. We were all pretty drunk, and I thought that maybe the whole conversation would be forgotten. So rather than show up and look like a fool, I just thought I'd skip the whole thing. Until O'Brien gave me a call asking where I was.

When I went there, I met with their president, a man by the name of C. W. Hannon. That's how I got a commission to design a bike that would be unveiled at the 1939 World's Fair in New York. It was the first time the world saw a real streamlined design. And they just loved it. Murray sold millions of those bikes.

I got into the pedal-car business right around the same time. I would sculpt full-sized models out of clay. And the engineers would decide whether or not it was economical to build.

Previous pedal cars were built like real cars, you know, with a body welded to a frame. But I designed mine so you could stamp the body out in a single piece over a die, and put different front ends and rear ends on them. It was more economical, and the designs were more realistic.

Children know detail. That's why we paid so much attention to detail in many of the designs; like the airplane had a propeller that turned as you moved, or the fire engine that had a bell that was like a real fire engine's bell. We had airplanes, fire engines, racecars, you name it.

> **That's how I got a commission to design a bike that would be unveiled at the 1939 World's Fair in New York. It was the first time the world saw a real streamlined design. And they just loved it. Murray sold millions of those bikes.**

We even had a pedal-car pirate version called the Jolly Roger. We actually got a complaint from some mother who said it wouldn't float. You know she tried it on some pond. But it didn't have a bottom. It just goes to show you how grownups' imaginations work.

Imagination — that's why I love toys. Even at my age, I still get them for my birthday. And that's what keeps me so young at heart.

When they had a show of all my work at the Cleveland Museum of Art a few years back, many people didn't know the breadth of my work, from watercolors and sculpture to pottery and industrial design. But I was more impressed with the number of people who brought in their old pedal cars for me to sign. It was very rewarding, knowing I had brought that much joy to so many people.

Viktor Schreckengost, industrial designer and artist. Photographed at his home in Cleveland Heights.

terry Stewart

I joined the Rock and Roll Hall of Fame and Museum just over five years ago and that's when I moved here. But during that short amount of time, I've found out what a fabulous place Cleveland is and how great its people are.

The really great thing about this city is that you can be a part of the fabric of the community, you can make a difference. You can live a diverse and rewarding life. And it's one that gives back on a daily basis. It asks and demands a lot of you in regard to people asking you to be involved in the community. But the payback is significant.

You can't say that about every city. I know, because I've lived in a few different towns and I've had several different careers.

I was with Marvel Comics, and a banker before that. I was also an engineer, and a lawyer on top of it all. I lived in New York City for many years and in Waterford, Connecticut. But I grew up in Alabama, so I've been around. I can tell you with some authority, Cleveland is one of the best places to live.

I can't say I'm fond of the weather, though. I guess every place has its trade-offs. The weather changes from day to day, even hour to hour, but the people and the community are a constant.

I do like the sunsets we have here in Cleveland. I live in Bratenahl, right on the lake and the sunsets are some of the best in the United States. And I'm close to downtown and work. I'm only eight minutes away, nine if it snows, 10 if there's an accident and 12 if we have both. Getting around in this town is really easy — you don't know how good you have it.

I've grown to love Cleveland's museums, the Art Museum, Natural History Museum, the HealthSpace museum and the Botanical Gardens. I never paid much attention to Cleveland's cultural amenities when I sought my job at the Rock Hall, but I have been pleasantly surprised.

All I knew five years ago was that I was trying to come to Cleveland for the greatest job possible. The folks at the Rock and Roll Hall of Fame and Museum didn't seek me out — I pursued them.

I had just left Marvel Comics in New York, and was doing some entertainment consulting when a friend of mine called and said he had found my next career. Since I never agree with him on anything, I decide to blow him off, but he told me to at least read the article in the *Wall Street Journal*.

I called him back after I read the article and told him, for once you're right. It was just buried in the paper, but I just knew I had to have the job. They had a search firm, and I wasn't sure who to contact.

So I just bombarded them — literally everyone I could think of — with résumés and letters.

Finally someone called and said, "Okay, that's enough, we got it. You want the job."

Luckily, they liked what I had to offer, so it was a fairly short process. I had my dream job. And it's been everything I thought it would be.

One of my first events here was actually a real highlight of my career. I don't go out of my way to meet celebrities or stars, but on occasion, I do have the need to speak with them or thank them for something they have donated or for their help on a project. Well one time, I had the occasion to meet Paul McCartney, only it was McCartney who introduced himself to me.

It was after an induction ceremony and Paul McCartney was at the Hall. We had an exhibit of some of his late wife's photos, and he had facilitated something and done some favors for the museum, so I was anxious to thank him.

I'm a big fan of clothes, always have been. So on this occasion I was wearing some pretty intense clothes. I saw him in the crowd and was starting to make my way over to him, but then I lost him. Then, out of nowhere, I felt this tug on my arm. It was Paul McCartney. He grabbed the lapel of my jacket and said, "Nice piece of shmata, young man," which of course is a Yiddish term for clothing or cloth. But that's how we met.

Of course, it was pretty cool meeting him that way, having him actually come up to me. But there have been other moments as well.

Then, out of nowhere, I felt this tug on my arm. It was Paul McCartney. He grabbed the lapel of my jacket and said, "Nice piece of shmata, young man," which of course is a Yiddish term for clothing or cloth.

Like I said, this is my dream job, so it's all pretty good.

Now my life is all about music, entertainment and pop culture. I enjoy listening to music, going to museums, attending plays and eating out. I'm still an avid collector, so I'm always on the lookout for records and memorabilia.

There's only one downside to my job at the Rock Hall and living in Cleveland. I simply don't have the time to do all the cultural things I enjoy doing here. There is so much to do in this city. I guess it's not really a negative.

It's just a lot more than I ever expected.

Finally someone called and said, "Okay, that's enough, we got it. You want the job."

Terry Stewart, President and CEO of the
Rock and Roll Hall of Fame and Museum.
Photographed at the Museum.

chuck Schodowski

When I started in television it was only supposed to be part time. And never, did I ever, want to be in front of the camera.

One night while driving down Pleasant Valley Road I looked up and saw the Channel 8 tower, and I started to daydream about working in television. You see, I never went to college. Like all the other Polish kids who lived on Cleveland's southeast side, I went to work in a foundry when I got out of high school. But my daydream of working in television just wouldn't leave me.

I went to Channel 3 because I heard they hired people as summer replacements part time. The chief engineer told me I needed to get a first-class FCC license, which was really just a nice way of blowing me off.

So, I went to school nights for three years and got my first-class FCC license. I went back to Channel 3 and the same guy was head engineer, so then he had to hire me as a summer replacement engineer. That's where I first met Ernie Anderson, who many know as Ghoulardi.

I worked at Channel 3 the summer of 1960, and the chief engineer thought I should stay in the business, so he gave someone at Channel 8 a call and I was hired on a temporary basis. I'd run audio or do switching, just about anything they'd want me to do. After three months, I went to the union steward and asked if I had a permanent position, and he said, "Only the station can tell you that. After six months, the union can do something about it, though." So I sweated out the next six months. But when I went back, they still couldn't tell me I was permanent.

In 1962, Channel 8 hired Ernie both as an announcer and to host a morning movie show. He brought this guy Tom Conway, who he wanted to be his director, which was a lie because all Tom did was write comedy sketches. And, of course, it was Tim Conway.

Anyway, we all got to be pretty good friends, and then Tom left to do the "Man on the Street" for Steve Allen and then "McHale's Navy." Then, in 1963, the station wanted Ernie to become the host of a Friday night horror movie and Ghoulardi was born. I used to write stuff for him, and I used to pick out all the music. The only kind of music Ernie liked was big band, and I had developed an appreciation for blues music working with black guys on the third shift of the foundry. So all the good bluesy music you heard on Ghoulardi, those were my records. But I still had no intention of ever getting in front of the camera. Hey, I still didn't know if I had a permanent position or not.

Then one day, I was switching audio and Ernie was sitting in the announcer booth, and we could see each other through the window. And he gets on the talk back and started asking me what size pants I wear and how big a shirt I need and what my hat size was. When I asked him why he said, "Because I need you to do a walk on for this skit." Afterwards, he was calling the Indians and getting my outfit, and I said, "There's no way you're getting me in front of the camera."

So he gets the three biggest guys on the set, and I mean these guys were big, and he said, "If you don't do it, these guys will persuade you to do it." So rather than try to fight them, I decided to do the skit, but boy was I nervous and scared. Which only added to the stupid skit.

I was supposed to be the Indians' new batting coach, and I was supposed to have come from the Mets, which were just a terrible team back then.

As a part of the skit, Ernie was interviewing me, and I was trying to give tips on hitting, but I couldn't hit the ball and each time I missed I would get more embarrassed and ticked off and Ernie kept trying to change the subject. It came across that he was trying to make an ass out of me — which was all a part of the skit, mind you — but people actually bought it and calls came into the station. They were complaining, "How could you treat this new guy with the Indians like that," and "How dare you do this to that nice young man," and Ernie just loved it, because it's exactly the kind of stuff Tom used to do with him. Pretty soon we did the same bit, only this time I was a judo instructor, or it would be some other sport and pretty soon the skits got easier and easier for me to do. I was working full time as an engineer, but I still didn't have anything permanent. I mean, I had three kids at home and I was really worried about it. But no one would tell me I was permanent.

Next thing you know, I became a regular on a skit called "Parma Place," which was a take off on Peyton Place, as handsome and debonair downstairs neighbor Jerry Kriegel. So for the next two years, I gave out autographs as Jerry.

> **You see, I never went to college. Like all the other Polish kids who lived on Cleveland's southeast side, I went to work in a foundry when I got out of high school. But my daydream of working in television just wouldn't leave me.**

Ernie actually gave me the nickname "Big Chuck." We used to play a lot of softball and basketball for the station back in those days. I used to hit a lot of home runs in softball, so Ernie started calling me "Big Chuck."

Ernie had a real thing about Parma. It was a running joke in the studio, just like the pink flamingos and the "certain ethnic" humor. He used to live there, you know, but he had moved out to Willoughby. After I was at the station for a while, I was looking for a house somewhere outside of Cleveland, and Ernie wanted me to move to Willoughby near him. Back in those days, the houses out there were too expensive for me. I finally settled on a home in Parma, and when I told Ernie, he kept going on and on about how stupid I was. I finally said, "Look Ernie, I have great neighbors on both sides of me, and I happen to like the town and the people, so don't knock Parma." Which, of course, was a mistake.

I knew that as soon as he was on the air, he would say something, so I told him, "Ernie, if you say anything about me being from Parma, the neighbors or pink flamingos, I'll cut your mike," and of course I could because I was running the audio. I knew I couldn't have any dead air

Big Chuck Schodowski, television personality.
Photographed on the set of the "Big Chuck and Li'l John Show."

time, so I made a tape of this Frankie Yankovich polka called "Who Stole the Kieshka." So every time he'd mention Parma, or pink flamingos, I would cut his mike and play the tape.

Ernie just loved it; whenever he heard the music he'd get up and start doing this crazy dance. It became a running gag. One time, he got on the air and told everyone that I could use a few extra pink flamingos for my lawn. Well, the next morning I woke up and there had to be 50 pink flamingos on my lawn. The kids watching must have stole every pink flamingo for miles around. I took them down to the station and they were all over the studio for months.

Of course, I also worked with Bob Wells, who many of you know as "Houlihan," and "Li'l John" Rinaldi, who's been my partner since 1979.

I can't even begin to tell you what a pleasure it has been working with those two. I'm sure we have more than 2,000 skits on tape, everything from the Kielbasa Kid to Ben Crazy — which is still popular with kids who don't know that it's a take off on the old Ben Casey show. My favorite was a Kielbasa Kid skit entitled "King the Wonder Dog." That's where the Kid is trapped under a fallen tree and King comes running to the rescue. Only he just jumps over the Kid and keeps on running. That won an Emmy. Actually it was the first Emmy ever awarded in Cleveland.

The 44 years I have been in television have been very rewarding, both in front of and behind the camera. But the real joke is that I'm still waiting for someone to tell me I have a permanent position.

I knew I couldn't have any dead air time, so I made a tape of this Frankie Yankovich polka called "Who Stole the Kieshka."

So every time he'd mention Parma, or pink flamingos, I would cut his mike and play the tape.

Ernie just loved it; whenever he heard the music he'd get up and start doing this crazy dance.

mike Belkin

f there's one sure thing in show business, it's that nothing's a sure thing. No matter how hot an artist is or how popular they are, you can still lose money. I learned that lesson right from the very beginning. There have been some shows where I got clobbered. I had one in Akron where I lost over a quarter of a million dollars. You have to put on a lot of winning shows to make up for that kind of money.

I grew up in Cleveland and have lived here all of my life. My family was in the clothing business and my dad owned a store on Ontario right near the old Central Market. My father was a shrewd businessman, very smart, and of course my mom was — well, she was the greatest mom in the world.

I started working there on Saturdays when I was seven years old, which I didn't really like because all my friends were playing baseball or basketball. But I had to go to the store with my mom and dad on Saturday because they both worked. I would dust the shoeboxes, or make suit boxes for a penny apiece. Then, when I was done working, I would walk up Ontario to Euclid Avenue and take the streetcar out to the corner of Euclid Heights Boulevard and Hampshire in Cleveland Heights. From there it was only a five-minute walk home.

By the time I was 10, I was already in sales. I remember one time a man came in who was interested in a pair of blue pants. I tried to help him, and he ended up leaving without buying anything. My father came over to me and asked what happened and I said, "He liked the blue pants, but said he would have to come back."

And my dad said, "I'm going to tell you a little story. I had the same thing happen to me yesterday. A man came in here, looked around and said he was going to come back. But as he left crossing the street, he got hit by a car, so he never came back." So I guess the moral of the story is that you better get the business while you can, or make hay while the sun shines.

Those are some of my fondest earliest memories.

I went off to college and even played professional baseball in the Texas League and the Big State League. I was signed by the Milwaukee Braves. But when I was through playing baseball, I came back here and my brother Jules and I opened a discount store in Painesville, as well as one in Ashtabula. In Ashtabula, we leased space from a building owner named Leroy Anderson (not the composer). He was a great promoter — he knew how to get people into our store. He did all kinds of promotions. One day he decided he was going to bring some talent into a ballroom restaurant in downtown Ashtabula, so he brought in Duke Ellington, then Louis Armstrong, then Lionel Hampton and people like that.

A lot of these artists he would make a few dollars on, and some he

would lose money on, and he probably did that for a year or so. Then I looked in the Cleveland paper to see what was happening here — and there really wasn't that much happening at all. So I said to Anderson and my brother Jules, "Why don't we try to do a concert in Cleveland and see what happens?"

We decided to bring in The Four Freshmen, so I called Capitol Records. At the time, The Four Freshmen were managed by Jerry Perenchio and their agent's name was Fred Dale, so I called him and told him I wanted to book the Four Freshmen and how much would it cost. He told me it would be $2,500 for the Four Freshmen. But then he asked, "Who's going to be your opening act? The Four Freshmen will play for an hour or an hour and fifteen — you need someone to open up for them." I asked him who he had, and he said a band called the New Christie Minstrels, which I thought was just great — of course that's where Kenny Rogers got his start. But at any rate, that was another $1,000 for them.

So we set the dates and I thought both of them on the same bill would be a great show. We were going to do the show at Music Hall, which is pretty small, so I said this is too big for only one show there, we have to do two shows. So we booked two shows, one at 7 p.m. and one at 9:30 p.m.

You understand that none of us knew anything about the concert business, but as they say, ignorance is bliss. Then we found out that we had to print tickets and sell tickets. Then we went down to the papers and they helped us put some ads together. Then there were costs for stagehands and printing — we were just winging it, but there was a cost at every turn. So we ran the ads, printed and sold the tickets and everything.

At any rate, we sold enough tickets at the door for the 9:30 show to cover our expenses and make a $65 profit — and that's what got us started.

When I tried to figure out how well we were doing in between shows, I found out we were losing $3,000. That amount of money isn't chopped liver today, but you can imagine what it was back then.

So I was sitting back on my chair, thinking, "Why did I ever do this? This was so stupid of me." And in walks my dad, and he asks me what's wrong. I tell him, "I can't believe I'm losing all this money!"

And he told me, "If you have a dream, son, sometimes you just have to do it." Which I really appreciated at the time. At any rate, we sold enough tickets at the door for the 9:30 show to cover our expenses and make a $65 profit — and that's what got us started."

Mike Belkin, promoter.
Photographed at the Music Hall, Cleveland.

patricia Heaton

guess I've always been performing — even when I was little. I used to write plays with my girlfriends in the neighborhood. We'd memorize all the musical albums my sisters brought home or that my parents had. And we'd often perform them, sometimes singing the entire score from movies like "Mary Poppins" — we did that on the swing sets of Normandy School. Other times we'd go over to the loading dock of the Heinen's supermarket across the street from our house and pretend it was a stage, singing themes from "Oliver" or "West Side Story" while on roller skates. Pretty dangerous when you think about it because there's nothing to keep you from going off the edge.

The first thing I ever did was a Christmas pageant. I was one of the angels who announced to the shepherds. Later I took acting classes at Huntington Playhouse in Bay Village. I did a couple of plays there when I was in eighth and ninth grade. I was in the chorus in both "Bells Are Ringing" and "Showboat." I wasn't exactly the leading lady, I just loved doing it.

But when I look back at Cleveland, it isn't about how I got my start in acting, or even some of those earliest performances — it's more about how much fun I had. I grew up on Midland Road in Bay Village in a fairly devout Catholic family. There were five of us kids, but my mother, who passed away when I was young, was one of 15 children. So I have a very extended family there. Sometimes it feels like I'm related to every fifth person there.

There was always a lot of laughter in our house. We weren't exactly poor, but we weren't rich either. But I was very lucky. My dad was a sportswriter, so he got free tickets. We used to get to do all kinds of cool stuff. We'd go to the Ice Capades, or see the Harlem Globetrotters. And every summer he'd take us to Cedar Point. Of course, growing up on Cleveland's West Side, that's almost a requirement of parenthood.

It was the mid-60s and my dad covered the Browns. That was back in the days of Jim Brown and Lou Groza and Bill Glass. They used to have their training camp out at Hiram College. Even though I was very small, my dad would take us out to the Browns' training camp with him in summer.

Even though we stayed in a real small dormitory room, it was still a big deal to me. There was something very exciting about eating all of your meals with the players and watching them practice — being able to run around on the field afterwards, and playing on all the equipment — you knew you were a part of something special.

That brings back memories of football season and fall. We used to rake huge leaf piles and then wrap someone in a blanket and throw them in a pile to see if they could get out. And in winter, we built the best snow forts ever. But summer was absolutely magical — decorating our bikes in red, white and blue crepe paper for the Fourth of July parade, picking elderberries down by the railroad tracks and baking them into pies. And games, we played them all: Capture the Flag, Hide and Seek, Red Light/Green Light, Hopscotch, Statues, and of course, Running Bases, which we played in the street.

That's what I like about Bay Village. You can probably still play on the street in certain neighborhoods and not worry about cars coming by.

I still get back there quite a bit, but not as much as I'd like. My husband likes to joke that I only go back when the weather's nice, but that's not true.

We came back for the holidays recently and it snowed on Christmas Eve. The snow was soft and thick on all the tree branches and roofs. It covered everything. The city looked like a postcard. We went sledding

> **I grew up on Midland Road in Bay Village in a fairly devout Catholic family. There were five of us kids, but my mother, who passed away when I was young, was one of 15 children. So I have a very extended family there.**

on Christmas Day — talk about bringing back some memories.

Of course, every time I'm back, it seems like there's never enough time. I always feel like I'm part of this big clan — maybe it's an Irish Catholic thing. But there are always cousins marrying friends of classmates, or baby showers or people you just have to see. Still, I always like going back.

Cleveland is my home. The town has some faults but it's always in my heart. If you're from Cleveland and you do something good, its people love you forever. ☕

If you're from Cleveland and you do something good, its people love you forever.

Patricia Heaton, actress.
Photographed in her dressing room on
the set of "Everybody Loves Raymond."

**m**y fondest memories of Cleveland are of growing up on Lakeview Road. It was an ethnic neighborhood and all of the families on Lakeview were very close — so close that we would call each other cousins, because calling someone a friend or neighbor just didn't get across how close the relationship was. There were apartments on Lakeview. Six or seven families would come out and share dinner on the weekends in the alley that ran behind the apartments.

The mothers would cook, the fathers would talk, my grandfather made wine. And we sang and ate. It was a wonderful experience.

I was baptized at Holy Rosary. I still like going back to that neighborhood on August 15 for the Feast of the Assumption. The sounds and smells of that celebration are a part of my life. When I was small, I knew all the cooks at all the stands because all the ladies knew my mother.

Nobody messed with the people in our neighborhood. If anyone saw somebody from the neighborhood in trouble, they wouldn't walk idly by. They'd put a stop to it fast. Everyone in the neighborhood watched out for each other and helped one another.

That's what impresses me most about Cleveland — its neighborhoods. We might not have the sophistication or commercial areas of cities of New York or Chicago, but Cleveland is a great place to live — especially if you're raising a family.

I went to Parkwood Elementary and Patrick Henry Junior High School. In my freshman year of high school I went to Cathedral Latin. It had a very profound impact on my life.

I played football there, quarterback. The lessons I learned playing football have stayed with me my entire life. Not just the athletic part, but the discipline — the way they treated you. It taught you teamwork. It taught you that you can't do everything by yourself. That if you try to do too much by yourself, you fail. You learn to depend on others, and if everybody does their job, it all works. It was a very important part of my basic education.

I liked history and art, but theology was my favorite subject. After football practice one day, one of the brothers at Cathedral Latin came up to me and said, "I'm thinking of forming a group of young people who I think may have a vocation, would you like to join?"

I had never thought about it before, but they convinced me to join. The more I learned about it, the more attractive it became. It eventually led to my ordination as a priest, which I still view as the greatest moment of my life. I was ordained at St. John Cathedral on May 23 and celebrated Mass the next day at Christ the King Parish in East Cleveland. Monsignor Shannon was the pastor, and my whole family was there. They flew in from all over the country. I remember thinking, this is sure a long way to come for a kid from Holy Rosary and Lakeview Road.

Those first years as a priest were spent in wonder and awe. It takes you a long time to realize what you are doing — you are just overwhelmed by it all. But you come to an understanding of it.

One great joy of being ordained in your hometown is that you get to baptize all your nephews and nieces and grand nephews and grand nieces — that was an especially happy part for me because our family is so close. Seeing all those children grow up has been a great joy.

Service and dedication to the church are a constant joy. But there are always reminders of what it really means. The sacrifices you have to make. It can literally cost you your life. I found that out in my first official act as Bishop of the Diocese of Cleveland.

It was a gray, dreary Cleveland day in November of 1980 in late afternoon. I had been named Bishop, but was not yet installed. I drove out to Cleveland Hopkins Airport with Mother Bartholomew of the Ursulines. We were greeted on the tarmac by some men who led us over to a plane. And when the cargo ramp of the plane opened, two baggage handlers rolled down two black-draped coffins. There was no fanfare, and very little said. But I knew the deceased well. I had worked with them.

Sister Dorothy Kazel and lay missionary Jean Donovan were martyred in El Salvador. When you consider the significance of what they did, and the sacrifice they made, it was very tragic. It gave me a very deep understanding about what it means to be in service and have dedication to the church. I'll certainly never forget it as long as I live.

But there were also bright spots. In the early '80s, I became deeply concerned about Catholic schools in the city, with the fear that we could no longer support a presence there for the children who needed us.

Nobody messed with the people in our neighborhood. If anyone saw somebody from the neighborhood in trouble, they wouldn't walk idly by. They'd put a stop to it fast

So I went out to the broader community, which had never been done. I felt these were assets not only for the Catholic Church, but for the whole community. So I tested the waters to see if corporate Cleveland, and others who were not part of the Catholic community, would share our concern and interest.

And they responded remarkably.

I presented them with what we were doing, and how well the children were doing, and with their help we were able to save 11 schools and the education of 7,000 children. Through the efforts of people like Bob Ginn, who is Episcopalian, Sam Miller, who is Jewish, and Kevin O'Donnell, who is Catholic, we raised more than $15 million — which was unheard of back then. There was hardly a corporation that didn't give something.

The whole community came together around us. For me, it has always had a lasting impact on the goodness of the people in this town.

Another thing I am especially proud of is our "Church and City"

Bishop Anthony M. Pilla,
Bishop of the Catholic Diocese of Cleveland.
Photographed at the Cathedral of
St. John the Evangelist.

initiative. We made a major effort to see what we could do to keep the 80-county diocese connected and mutually responsive. Again, we were losing a presence in urban centers like Lorain, Akron and Cleveland because everyone was moving to the suburbs. Yet the people who were left behind were the people who needed us most because they didn't have the resources to move. When we had to close or leave, the whole neighborhood would deteriorate. And we couldn't be there without the support of the suburban entities.

Again, I wasn't sure how the initiative would go. But it worked. Again the people in the broader community responded remarkably. After a major effort that has lasted 10 years, our suburban parishes have linked up with urban parishes and formed partnerships. We realize that the presence of the Church, and Catholic schools in particular, is a critical component of the stability of the neighborhoods in the city.

We had to overcome a lot of tensions to get it to work, but everyone came together for the sake of everybody. There is a lot of talk about regionalism now—that was a regional effort.

That's what I truly like best about the City of Cleveland. I'm a native, so I naturally love it. But I've also found that there are just good people here, throughout the whole area and in our neighborhoods in the city. If you give them good information for a legitimate cause, they will always respond.

I don't think you'll find that everywhere.

But there are always reminders of what it really means. The sacrifices you have to make. It can literally cost you your life. I found that out in my first official act as Bishop of the Diocese of Cleveland.

The lessons I learned playing football have stayed with me my entire life. Not just the athletic part, but the discipline—the way they treated you. It taught you teamwork. It taught you that you can't do everything by yourself.

mal Mixon

've read some recent editorials that say the entrepreneurial spirit is disappearing in Cleveland. That's just not true. Cleveland was once home to people like John D. Rockefeller, Samuel Mather and Charles Brush, and while we might not have people of that stature in our community today, I can assure you we do have a lot of entrepreneurs.

I have always been an admirer of entrepreneurial spirit, of new ideas and of creating something out of nothing. I know what I'm talking about because when I came here from Oklahoma, I really had no money or family connections. To be truthful, the only reason I came here is because I met my wife Barbara at Wellesley and she was an Ohio girl, so I thought I'd move here to please her. Besides, there wasn't much to do back in Oklahoma.

I had graduated Harvard, where I received what amounted to a full scholarship in return for four years of military service. I chose the Marine Corps option and went to Vietnam in 1965 and '66. When I came back I went back to Harvard Business School.

But then, like I said, I followed my wife to Cleveland. I took a good job with Harris Corporation. Later I worked with another company called Technicare, and that's really when I got the idea to go out on my own.

Johnson & Johnson bought Technicare; Invacare was a subsidiary that had been for sale for three years. No one wanted to buy it for the price they were asking. Johnson & Johnson put it on waivers, but had no takers. So it was kind of an orphan.

I had made friends with the technical genius at Technicare, J.B. Richey, and he wanted to go off and form our own company. Johnson & Johnson was asking $8 million for Invacare. All I needed at the time was $7,990,000 because I had a whopping $10,000 of seed money.

So from that humble beginning I was able to raise the necessary funds in what were very difficult economic times. It was the end of 1979, and by the time 1980 rolled around, interest rates were right around 26 percent. But we raised a million dollars for common stock and another half a million of preferred stock, and then borrowed the balance of the $7.8 million purchase price. So my $10,000 investment is today worth well over $100 million. And the company we bought for $7.8 million has a market equity cap of about $1.4 billion, and with debt that could easily be as high as $1.6 billion to $1.7 billion.

I've been involved with other start-ups as well. I helped my friend John Balch buy Royal Appliance, and we built the Dirt Devil brand, taking the company public. All told, I have been involved with 25 or 30 companies over the years. And I still hold private investments in a number of private companies in the Greater Cleveland area. One of the things I am most proud of is creating a venture fund that raised $25 million for African American entrepreneurs with the idea of creating more wealth in that community.

I'm also involved with a number of civic organizations and serve on the board of directors for a number of companies and organizations. But I'm always looking for the next deal.

Cleveland is home to some of the best cultural organizations in the nation. We have an excellent art museum, more live theater than just about any city this side of the Mississippi except New York, and an orchestra that is without equal anywhere in the world. And while I do like to relax now and then, I still spend my weekends pouring over deals. My wife thinks I'm crazy.

> **One of the things I am most proud of is creating a venture fund that raised $25 million for African American entrepreneurs with the idea of creating more wealth in that community.**

It's not so much about earning, or compensation. You reach a point and all of that becomes secondary. The thing is, I know how to take any company and make it better. How to put together a good board and a good management team.

Some people have hobbies, others collect art. For me, it's the art of the deal. I enjoy meeting new entrepreneurs, in seeing new thinking and what's going on in the world.

That's how I remain active. And that's also how I know the entrepreneurial spirit is alive and well here in Cleveland.

I have always been an admirer of entrepreneurial spirit, of new ideas and of creating something out of nothing.

A. Malachi Mixon III, Chairman of the Board
and Chief Executive Officer, Invacare Corporation.
Photographed at his office in Elyria.

katharine lee Reid

art and life have always been synonymous to me. I had the great good fortune to grow up with a kind of an insider's view of creative inspired expression, and I savored it as it shaped my way of seeing of the world and created a vision that stays with me to this day.

I was 10 years old when my family moved to Cleveland from Seattle in 1952. It was an era when the workplace was still largely the domain of men. Most women viewed themselves primarily as wives and mothers, and they expected that their daughters would follow a similar path.

For the most part, I fit the mold — except perhaps for the occasional secret cigarette with my pal next door, with whom I'd sneak up to the vacant lot and literally blow smoke at the idea of "good little girls."

I also tapped my share of trees in that lot in search of "fresh" maple syrup, but that's about as rebellious as I got. Even then, I was acutely aware of the aesthetics of my surroundings: the shimmering silver grays of the tree trunks with their amber sap.

Our home was five minutes from the Cleveland Museum of Art, where my dad, Sherman E. Lee, as a graduate student taught Saturday art classes and years later became director in 1958. We lived among Japanese, Chinese and Indian art, as well as European and American paintings. In fact, one of the screens that used to hang above our sofa is now in the Museum's Japanese collection.

Those works of art were almost like members of our family, resulting in a few embarrassing moments when I would invite friends over to the house. My father had a special admiration for Indian sculpture and one extremely well-endowed female deity in our living room greeted each guest in the nude.

As I grew older, I frequented the Heights Art Theater at Coventry, where I gave my heart to a gallant actor named Humphrey Bogart. I also loved Jacques Tati and Fernandel movies; they were France's answer to Buster Keaton and Charlie Chaplin.

I can never forget my art classes at the Museum with Ms. Wike and later with Mr. Day, whose class was both challenging and gentle. He was serious about the creative process, and it was memorable to be one of his students. But I first remember creating crayon copies of the Kandinskys on display in a 1952 exhibition here. That was my introduction to modern art, and I never saw the world quite the same again. Although I have developed a special interest in Old Masters, I continue to have a special love for the art of our time.

In the ninth grade, we devoted an entire year to studying Cleveland. The project required us to present an overview of an institution of our choosing. Of course, I chose the Museum. The Museum then comprised only the original 1916 building and I solemnly observed that the Museum needed more space. Nearly a half a century and three new wings later the Museum's leadership reached the same conclusion in the 1999 Master Plan: We needed more space to display the art as well as better amenities for the public.

Those memories remain precious. Most of all, I remember Dad sticking his head into the Museum library, where I often studied during vacations from college, and asking, "Want to see the new acquisitions?"

I loved Dad's wide-ranging view for the history of cultures and art in particular. He had a real grasp of the whole stream of human creativity and strategically modeled the collection with extraordinary works that completed that vision.

But Dad was focused on the style that made each work unique and was much less interested in the story behind the piece itself and that was something I always wanted to know. I think that's the difference in our perspectives. From my early years with the wonders of the Cleveland collection, I've always felt strongly about all of the stories behind a work of art. When these are expressed visually by imaginative artists, they are given a force and uniqueness that truly moves people. That realization has shaped my vision more than anything else.

As I entered the professional arena, women's liberation was dawning and the idea of being a wife and mother seemed at the time less fulfilling for me personally than pursuing my own vision. But I quickly discovered that only my optometrist cared much about the vision of a young woman in the art world of the '60s.

By the time I arrived at the Art Institute of Chicago in 1982, I was fully entrenched in my personal liberation from "doing things Dad's way." Still, after nearly a decade there and even after becoming a deputy director, I realized I still wasn't doing things my way. My husband, Bryan, told me that I would never be happy until I ran my own museum. He was right.

But I first remember creating crayon copies of the Kandinskys on display in a 1952 exhibition here. That was my introduction to modern art, and I never saw the world quite the same again.

I became director of the Virginia Museum of Fine Art in 1991. By then, I'd learned that simply contemplating my vision wasn't enough. The key was involving others, both the staff and community, in it and giving them ownership to test it and strengthen it. We transformed the presentation of the entire museum that way.

When I returned home to direct The Cleveland Museum of Art in 1999, the memories behind the walls were as real to me as the paintings on them. I remember most how my two sisters and my brother and I would walk through the collection on Dad's wing-tipped heels like four little ducklings as Papa duck strode through the galleries and storerooms showing us with delight the latest find.

Today, I walk those same galleries in my own shoes and share ownership of my own vision with others who are helping to strengthen it and see it come to fruition. ⌒

Katharine Lee Reid, Director, The Cleveland Museum of Art.
Photographed at the Museum.

alex Machaskee

I wrote my first byline story when I was 15 years old, so I got into the newspaper business at a pretty young age. I got injured playing football, and later basketball, and developed what is known as Osgood Slaughter's disease in the knee. I couldn't play sports for a while, so I called the sports editor at *The Warren Tribune* and asked if I could get a part-time job.

I worked on sports through high school, starting out at 20 hours a week as a sophomore. By the time I was a senior, I was working 40 hours a week. Eventually, I became a general assignment reporter and covered everything but the society news.

Having a pretty solid background of writing experience, I went to a recruitment firm and they told me that there was an opening in the promotion department of *The Plain Dealer*. Had I been reading the classified section back then I would have seen that *The Plain Dealer* was advertising for the opening, and I would have saved my $375. But I guess that's water under the bridge. So that's how I came to Cleveland.

In my 43 years here in Cleveland, first in promotion, later as director of labor relations and eventually as publisher of *The Plain Dealer,* I have many fond memories. But I suppose the one that really sticks out is the one I cut my teeth on in promotion. It was the latter half of 1962, so it's going back a little ways, to the days of the Kennedy administration and the space race.

We came up with the idea to do a three-day Space Science Fair, cooperating with NASA here in town, and somehow the idea caught on in Washington at NASA's headquarters. The event eventually ballooned into a nine-day show that was free to the public. I remember it well because I put so much effort into the event. The part I remember most was the night before it opened.

We were having a black tie dinner at the Renaissance Hotel, which back then was the Sheraton. We were going to be the first event held in their new ballroom — but it was still under construction. I remember going over there just before the dinner, watching them lay the carpet, that's just how close it was. Needless to say, everything came together.

The Space Fair itself was a huge success. It drew more than 375,000 people to Public Hall. We even had a five-day, Monday through Friday, Space Institute for school children and more than 55,000 students got bused in for classes that were taught by NASA personnel. It was a lot of effort and anxiety, but it all came off well.

We were going to be the first event held in their new ballroom—but it was still under construction. I remember going over there just before the dinner, watching them lay the carpet, that's just how close it was.

Since then I've been involved in numerous civic events. I recently chaired the renovation of Severance Hall, which had not been touched for 66 years. Any time you do a physical renovation, there's a chance that the acoustics may be destroyed. I can't begin to tell you the exhilaration I felt when I first heard the orchestra three and a half years later when the renovation was complete. Being a musician, I got a lot of personal satisfaction out of that.

I'm also very proud of what we've been able to do here at *The Plain Dealer,* with our new production facility on Tiedeman Road and our brand-new offices downtown. Both of those events are very special, and from a professional standpoint are probably much more significant than my first major promotional event. But I will always remember the Space Fair. It was a coming-out party for both NASA and *The Plain Dealer.* And it was my baptismal to the world of promotions.

Had I been reading the classified section back then I would have seen that *The Plain Dealer* was advertising for the opening, and I would have saved my $375.

Alex Machaskee, Publisher, President and CEO of The Plain Dealer. *Photographed at the newspaper's Tiedeman Road Plant.*

al Roker

When I first came to Cleveland, I thought I was stepping into a scene out of Dante's Inferno. It was back in November of 1983, and I remember flying into Cleveland Hopkins Airport and taking a cab to an interview I had for a job at WKYC-TV. I had grown up in Brooklyn and Queens in New York, so I was used to the city, but I wasn't used to seeing the steel mills, which were still going pretty strong back then.

I was married to someone else at the time, and when I saw the flames leaping from the tops of the smokestacks I thought, "My God, she's going to think we're stepping into a scene from hell." I had been in broadcasting in smaller cities, but this was my chance to break into a Top 10 market. To be truthful, I would have taken the job even if they were performing human sacrifices on Public Square.

As I came into downtown, I was really expecting the worst — broken sidewalks and cars on fire, but what I saw was a really quaint downtown. It was quiet. There weren't a lot of people. But there was also very little crime.

I soon found out that Cleveland is a great place just to hang out. I lived in Shaker Heights and used to enjoy going to Thornton Park. On weekends, I loved going down to the lake, east side or west side — it's just beautiful. A lot of my memories in Cleveland revolve around eating. I liked Tommy's in Cleveland Heights and a restaurant called Noggin's in Shaker, and I used to go to Yours Truly. In the Flats I went to Sammy's for fine dining. I also used to hang at Rick's Cafe in Chagrin Falls. But one of the best memories I have is going to the West Side Market and experiencing all the smells, sounds and tastes of everything there.

The thing I like most about Cleveland is the openness of its people. They are not duplicitous. They'll tell you what they think. They will either take you to their bosom, or will chew you up and spit you out pretty quickly. What is interesting is that you are not really considered a part of the city until you have been there about five years. The funny thing is, I could have stayed in Cleveland for 30 years and I would have been a newcomer compared to Dick Goddard, who is the dean of Cleveland weathermen and one of the legendary weather forecasters in the country. He was a great mentor.

So I guess I don't really have any one single favorite memory of Cleveland. But it was a coming of age for me. I guess that's why I'm so fond of the town. I achieved my first success in Cleveland, and people today still think I'm from the city because I talk it up so much. My sister lives there now along with her husband and my nephew and two nieces, so I get back there a fair amount.

What I didn't know is that once you have been in Cleveland five years, you're a part of a family. They'll never let you go. I had just become a part of that family when I got the opportunity to join the "Today" show in New York.

The first time I came back was about a year after I had left. I had gotten in a cab at Hopkins and the cabbie looks at me and says, "Hey, how ya been?" and then says, "So what, are you coming back from vacation?"

And I said, "Well I don't live here anymore."

The thing I like most about Cleveland is the openness of its people. They are not duplicitous. They'll tell you what they think. They will either take you to their bosom, or will chew you up and spit you out pretty quickly.

And he said, "But I just saw you on TV. I saw you a couple of mornings ago."

I told him that I worked on the "Today" show, and he said, "Hey, if you don't want to tell me where you're coming back from vacation, well that's okay."

So you see, Cleveland won't let go of you once you're accepted. Which is nice. It's nice to have two homes.

What I didn't know is that once you have been in Cleveland five years, you're a part of a family. They'll never let you go.

Al Roker, meteorologist.
Photographed on the set of NBC's "Today" in Manhattan.

adele Malley

I love being in the chocolate business, but it was really my husband Bill who grew the business. And it wouldn't have been possible without the Clevelanders who supported so much of what we did. I guess that's why I love Cleveland so much.

But my fondest memories are of growing up in Fairview Park. I was raised right over the Metropolitan Park by Mastick Road and spent most of my childhood playing on the hills down there. In spring, an older gentleman from the neighborhood would come by our house and take everyone on a hike. You could watch the world renew itself, the violets and trilliums blooming.

Cleveland's Emerald Necklace has always meant a great deal to me. I still like to drive through the Metroparks to see each new season. It's a nice way to relax and get back on track as to what's really important in your life. Most cities don't have that.

When I was a child, Fairview Park was on the outskirts of town. If you played a game of baseball against somebody in Fairview Park and rode your bicycle out there, you felt like you were riding out to the country. At least that's what my husband Bill tells me.

Bill, of course, grew up in the candy business. But I grew up in a family business too. So there's some entrepreneurial spirit in my background as well. My father, Bill Ryan, ran the Bill Ryan Provision Company on East Fourth and Bolivar — which now is right about second base at Jacobs Field. He catered to the ships on the Great Lakes. He died when I was in sixth grade and my mother, Adele Ryan, took over the business. Her name was just like mine, but everyone knew her as Daisy.

She kept the business alive for my brothers, and became quite a businessperson in her own right — all at a time when career women were almost unheard of.

After my father died, my mother had no one to confide in except us kids. So my two brothers and I grew up listening to the business. She would come home and talk about the business, and we helped her in any way we could.

When a parent dies, there is a coming together that is very different from when both parents are there. You form this protective barrier, and there is a lot more work for you to do. Both my brothers went on to be successful businessmen in their own right.

I became very close with my mother growing up. She was just a real neat person and we used to have a good time together because we liked the same things.

She is the one who introduced me to Malley's Chocolates.

When I was young we would drive down to the Malley's store on Madison Avenue and look in their window. And it was just so fetching and beautiful — like every day was Christmas. We used to go there for special treats and things. Of course, I never knew then that one day Bill Malley would be the love of my life.

I met Bill in early fall of 1957. I was on a blind date with another fellow and Bill cut in on a dance.

Bill lived in Lakewood at the time, two doors down from the old Lakeshore Hotel on Lake Avenue. Bill lived with a group of bachelors who had rented out one of the large mansions down there. There must have been eight bedrooms in that house, and all the bachelors had different rooms. They all ate together and lived together — it was interesting to see how they lived.

And they had the best parties. I met Bill at one of those parties. After Bill cut in on a dance, he went up to this other fellow and talked to him.

He called soon after that and we started dating. It wasn't long after that I decided I really liked him.

My mother and I would drive to the Malley's store and look at him while he was working because I was trying to decide about him. He would sit in a booth in the store doing the books and late at night we'd drive by and see him sitting there.

He always worked late, getting out of work at close to midnight, then he'd come over to our house. And the way he would soften his appearance at that hour was by bringing my mother's favorite ice cream — which was fudge ripple. So we would sit around and eat ice cream late at night and talk.

During the holidays I would always get chocolate. One Easter I got this huge chocolate bunny. Well, I came home that night, right after Bill had given me the bunny, and it was sitting in the kitchen. But all around the base there were nicks and pieces of it missing. And my mother said, "I'm sorry Adele, but I just couldn't resist. I could smell it all the way from my room."

There's something about the sweet smell of chocolate — it's just irresistible. But so was Bill.

Bill lived with a group of bachelors who had rented out one of the large mansions down there. There must have been eight bedrooms in that house, and all the bachelors had different rooms. They all ate together and lived together — it was interesting to see how they lived.

Bill and I were married in 1959, and I've been in the chocolate business ever since. And it's been a good life. Like I said, Clevelanders supported so much of what we did — and for that I am truly grateful.

It meant we could grow the business. It was delightful to watch because we were also able to employ those children who wanted to be a part of the business.

Of course, we're both retired now. But we're thoroughly happy with how we progressed. It took a lot of work, and it took a lot of thought. But it's all been very sweet — if you'll pardon the pun. ➥

CORDIAL
CHERRIES
DARK CHOCOLATE
$5.95
8.25 OZ (177g)

NUTMALLOW
CHUNKS
MILK CHOCOLATE
$10.95
PER POUND

ANUT BUTTER
TRUFFLE
.95

TRUFFLE
COCONUT
$16.95
PER POUND

TRUFFLE
BLACK
RASPBERRY
$16.95
PER POUND

TRUFFLE
STRAWBERRY
CHEESECAKE
$16.95
PER POUND

Adele Malley, retired CEO, Malley's Chocolates.
Photographed at the chocolate factory
in Brook Park, Ohio.

CORDIAL
CHERRIES
MILK CHOCOLATE
$16.95
PER POUND

CORDIAL
CHERRIES
DARK CHOCO

TIRAM

$16.95

ALMOND
CRUNCH
MILK CHOCOLATE

ORANGE
PEELS

OR
P

michael Benz

You want to know what's really great about Cleveland? Clevelanders. They are diverse. They are caring. They are driven. The strength of any community is in its people. We have great leaders. We have great workers. And we have great innovators. A lot of "firsts" have come out of Cleveland.

I am very positive about the things that have happened here, and I saw this city when it was on its knees. We've had our share of challenges, but we've picked ourselves up by our bootstraps. When the city went into default, we didn't go for the federal bailout. When we had an image problem, we didn't turn away. The community rallied together to start solving problems and taking advantage of opportunities.

It's people like George Voinovich, Dick Pogue, Albert Ratner, Alex Machaskee, Tom Vail and others who took on these challenges. People like Bill Bryant, my former boss at the Growth Association, and all the entrepreneurs at COSE. Risk takers who put it on the line every day.

Everything that I have been involved with in this community has been about people coming together to make a difference. Whether it was the Growth Association, COSE, the Rock and Roll Hall of Fame and Museum or my work here at United Way, it's not just about one person with an idea, but people rallying around — people who are good with finance, or good with development, or good with architecture. People in this community do not stand around wringing their hands saying "Woe is me," they come together and do something about it.

That's how COSE started. It started out of a problem, a truck strike in the early '70s. It was when small businesses, not only here, but across the country, didn't have a voice. People took small businesses for granted. Out of that developed a need. So small businesses here got together and started working for themselves and the community. We had a professional staff, but it was really our volunteer leaders who addressed the problems small businesses had in government. We came together as a team and as a board. That's how everything happened.

I was hired at the Growth Association in 1970. It was a great early laboratory to learn in. If I had to pick one of the most fulfilling projects of my career, it would be my work with COSE. It's what honed my entrepreneurial skills, not just in business, but in nonprofit organizations. I was a young buck back then and we tried some pretty crazy stuff. One of the first seminars we ever ran at COSE was, "How To Screw Uncle Sam Out of Tax Dollars." Boy did I get nailed for that title. Dick Adler, who was our executive vice president back then, called me down and said, "Mike, we can't do this."

Well, we had a huge turnout. The thing about it was we weren't trying to cheat the government, we were just trying to help small businesses manage their taxes. It was put on by a major local accounting firm, and they stressed paying your fair share, but also how not to pay more than you should. It taught me that people would come together. That these small business entrepreneurs were drivers.

The other thing I'm very proud of is my involvement in helping Cleveland land the Rock and Roll Hall of Fame and Museum. It all started as an idea I got from an article someone wrote in *Crain's Cleveland Business.* We decided to build a community-wide team to win it. Nobody even knew it existed until we got in the game. We had been in the running for four or five months and no one knew we were in the game except for the people in New York. Then a public announcement was made by the Rock and Roll Hall of Fame Foundation in New York City that Cleveland was interested in being the site of the Rock and Roll Hall of Fame. At that time, New York Mayor Koch was going to donate a brownstone in Manhattan to house the museum—then, at the last minute, communities from around the country became interested.

The fun and craziness of helping to bring all that together was the highlight of my career. It was the excitement of getting Clevelanders behind it and believing in it. We almost lost it and we had to go back a second time, which was very traumatic. We had to raise $60 million, but the community rallied around and we built a world-class building designed by I.M. Pei.

I remember sitting in New York when they made the final announcement and they said what won it for Cleveland was Clevelanders. Everybody contributed, and during the process, all egos were checked at the door.

> **I remember sitting in New York when they made the final announcement and they said what won it for Cleveland was Clevelanders. Everybody contributed, and during the process, all egos were checked at the door.**

Now, when I go down to the Rock Hall, it's almost like home. I played a role, but the role I played was that of an organizational manager. I simply organized the resources of the entire community — there were no Lone Rangers on that project.

Of course, coming to the United Way has been another thrill because when I first came here, it seemed as though we had lost our way. But it's been a real thrill to be president of an institution that has made significant progress and has leadership at all levels.

As I said before, Cleveland is successful and it will continue to be successful because of Clevelanders. This is the most philanthropic city, person for person, of any city in the country. And that's why I'm so proud to be from Cleveland.

Michael Benz, President and CEO,
United Way Services of Cleveland.
Photographed at E. 9th and Lakeside.

ray Shepardson

What's so amazing about Cleveland is that an outsider like myself, with substantially no worth —just a good idea and some enthusiasm — was so well received. The accessibility I gained to high society in Cleveland was nothing short of remarkable. That accessibility made saving Playhouse Square possible.

However, no production would be possible without the people behind the scenes. My friendship with Adrian "Junior" Short made saving Playhouse Square a reality.

I was brought to Cleveland by Paul W. Briggs, who was the superintendent of Cleveland Public Schools back in the '60s. I was attending Seattle Pacific College and Paul came out to visit his son in the Army who was stationed at Fort Lewis.

I met Paul at what can only be described as an accidental lunch. He invited me and my roommate Dave to come to Cleveland for an interview. Dave played hard to get, but I got excited. I guess that's what got me here. I became special assistant to Paul Briggs.

I learned more in my two years with Paul Briggs than I did in my previous 18 years of schooling. He was like a father to me and a great mentor. I brought in visiting scholars for the district. Bill Cosby came in to help us integrate the schools. We had a couple of astronauts. And I had Buckminster Fuller for a whole week.

That's when I got the idea to try to save the theatres of Playhouse Square. When Bucky Fuller came in as a part of the visiting scholars program he egged me on to do something big enough to make a difference — to not just save one theatre, but all of them.

As I started to put the project together (and I spent more than a year doing it), I became increasingly discouraged. I contacted the folks at Halle's Department Store for support, and was told that the only Halle crazy enough to help me was Kay Halle — but she lived in Washington, D.C.

She had made quite a name for herself as a great Washington hostess, connecting politicians with intellectuals. She was the lady who, when Jack Kennedy was elected, brought in artists and intellectuals for the inauguration and arranged for them to stay in the homes of politicians. She was a great friend to Averell Harriman, who was governor of New York, and Alice Roosevelt Longworth, Teddy's daughter, who was the grand dame of Washington society. I thought that she, if anyone, would be able to help me.

I found out she was in town speaking at the Western Reserve Historical Society. After her speech I went up, introduced myself and told her about my plan to save the theatres.

"Do you have a car, darling?" she asked. "I'm going to dump these museum people and take you up the hill to meet the next governor of the State of Ohio."

It was a benefit for Jack Gilligan. Kay and I hit it off pretty well. Toward the end of the evening she said to me, "I can't help you the way

I would like to because I live in Washington. But there is a lady here who is my counterpart. She will do for you what I would do for you if you lived in Washington."

Kay Williams had a bit of a speech impediment; sometimes, you could hardly understand her. I went to a couple of her parties and we were just getting acquainted when I got a call.

I was still with the Board of Education, and working late. That's back when the Met used to play Public Auditorium. They always had a dinner before called the Pavilion that was all black tie and fancy, the society thing. So it's six o'clock and Kay calls me up and says, "I want you to meet some people, so just come across the street."

And I say, "But Kay, I'm wearing Sansabelt slacks and a polyester blazer with loafers, how can I..."

"Anyone," she says, cutting me off, "anyone who will care how you are dressed doesn't matter."

So I went over, but I have to tell you I would have been more comfortable in a waiter's uniform. That was Kay, and that's why she was such an incredible hostess.

Kay Williams took me under her wing and introduced me to everybody who is anybody. I went to her parties and every five minutes she grabbed me and introduced me to someone else. I met the CEOs of all the banks, as well as a lady by the name of Lainie Hadden, who is the true savior of Playhouse Square. At first Lainie thought I was a bit of a flim-flam man. It took her a year or two to find out that I was real.

I often look back on my first encounter with Junior Short. That confrontational, magical accident is like the story of my life.

So it was that kind of access which led to what is now Playhouse Square. The Junior League backed the first production of "Jacques Brel is Alive and Well and Living in Paris," directed by Joe Garry and starring the marvelous Providence Hollander, David Frazier, Terry Piteo and Cliff Bemis. That was 31 years ago.

But none of it would have been possible without the help of my friend Junior Short. He is the forgotten man of Playhouse Square — a tough union organizer and a boss. He was a visionary who understood that Playhouse Square would be a source of jobs for stagehands forever.

He protected me in the early days and made so many things possible. Things that no one really knew anything about. It was his support and vision in the formative years of Playhouse Square that allowed us to survive and thrive.

But our friendship started out on a rocky note.

Our first encounter was backstage at the Allen Theatre. We had an argument over the grand drape, which deteriorated into a nose-to-nose yelling match. It almost came to fisticuffs. I went home shaking because he was a very powerful man. But from that day on we were best friends.

He was a little guy, but he had a presence about him. You just knew

Ray Shepardson, preservationist
and theatre restoration consultant.
Photographed at the Genessee Theatre
in Waukegan, Illinois.

he was one tough son of a bitch. He had a full head of hair, a stocky build and a firm jaw. Today his son Tom is president of the International and his other son, Dale, who is also a fine attorney, is the business manager.

Junior Short got me the best stagehands. Our union negotiations would consist of 20 minutes shooting the breeze before we got down to business. Then he'd say, "Let's get down to business. Here's what I have in mind."

And I'd say, "That looks good to me."

And we'd be done.

He was fair but firm. It was a wonderful friendship, but no one really knows anything about it.

Without the support of people like the Haddens, Halles and people like Kay Williams, Playhouse Square would have never been possible. But without the relationship with the stagehands and organized labor, I never would have been able to survive. You don't see the stagehands, but they are the ones who make extraordinary things happen on stage.

I often look back on my first encounter with Junior Short. That confrontational, magical accident is like the story of my life. I've had an unbelievably lucky existence, falling into relationships and happenings.

All of my life, I've been able to live off the inspiration of unbelievable people who I just keep running into.

Our first encounter was backstage at the Allen Theatre. We had an argument over the grand drape, which deteriorated into a nose-to-nose yelling match. It almost came to fisticuffs. I went home shaking because he was a very powerful man. But from that day on we were best friends.

But none of it would have been possible without the help of my friend Junior Short. He is the forgotten man of Playhouse Square — a tough union organizer and a boss. He was a visionary who understood that Playhouse Square would be a source of jobs for stagehands forever.

george Stephanopoulos

throughout my childhood, I had always wanted to become a priest. You see, someone in my family had always been a priest. But sometimes an expectation nurtured through childhood can come undone in a single moment.

It was the autumn of 1974, right after my family had moved from New York to Cleveland. I was sitting in homeroom at Orange High School shortly before eight, when I got the idea that I just wanted to be one of the guys. I hadn't lost my faith, but I had lost interest in becoming a priest and carrying on the family legacy.

So I became one of the guys, sneaking into golf courses, playing poker with the money I earned from all of my part-time jobs. It seemed like I was always working when I was in high school. I worked at the Chagrin Valley Country Club as a caddy, washed dishes at the Pepper Pike Country Club, and worked as a busboy at Executive Caterers. It's a pretty big stretch going from a busboy to working for the President and hosting your own television show. I guess my point is that Cleveland is where I learned how to work hard.

A good part of that work ethic came from being a wrestler. I wrestled the entire time I was in high school. Played soccer too. It's amazing how central sports and activities are to community life in the Cleveland area. But wrestling was tough. I'll never forget the first practice. It was murder. My mom came to pick me up afterward. I wanted to quit, but she made me stick it out. I'm still grateful to this day.

Not that I was all that great. I lost my first match 19-2, and never caught up after that. But wrestling is a sport that teaches you discipline. It's really all about the impact the sport had on me rather than what I did on the mat.

That first year, I was a pretty chubby kid, but well coordinated. I weighed 120 pounds in September, but wanted to wrestle at 98, so I had to cut weight.

Talk about work. I ran before school, dieted on oranges, and exercised at night. That was back when they allowed you to practice and run in plastic suits. By the time November came around I weighed 98, but it took a lot of work — more than you can imagine. Wrestling taught me the power of self-discipline and exercise. For that, I am truly grateful.

I did other things in high school as well. As I said, I played soccer, but I also worked on the yearbook. It wasn't until later that I was bitten by the political bug. My first political job was for local Judge Joseph Nahra. He was a family friend, and I went door-to-door handing out leaflets. I really caught the bug when I worked with former Congresswoman Mary Rose Oakar as a summer intern in 1981. My first real job was working for Congressman Ed Feighan. I was working for Dick Gephardt in 1991, when he decided not to run for president. That's how I came to work for the Clinton campaign. I guess everyone kind of knows the story from there.

In Cleveland I learned some very valuable lessons — the importance of having discipline and a good work ethic. It's something that people from Cleveland seem to have. It's something I carry with me to this very day.

Looking back, I loved everything about going to high school in Cleveland. Orange High School was a terrific school. I made many friends there. Friends I still have to this day. I even make it back once in a while, when I can, to visit old friends and reminisce, or go to the Tick Tock Tavern for ribs — which are still my favorite.

In Cleveland I learned some very valuable lessons — the importance of having discipline and a good work ethic. It's something that people from Cleveland seem to have. It's something I carry with me to this very day.

I loved everything about going to high school in Cleveland. Orange High School was a terrific school. I made many friends there. Friends I still have to this day.

George Stephanopoulos, anchor of ABC News' "This Week."
Photographed on the set of the show in Washington, D.C.

sister juanita Shealey

Whenever I meet someone new, I'm always happy when they tell me who they are without telling me what they do for a living. What you do for a living is important and it takes a large slice of your life — but it's not you. If you're a doctor, you're not just a doctor, you're so much more than that. If you're a teacher, you're not just a teacher, you're so much more than that. The same can be said of many professions.

So when anybody ever asks me who I am, and a lot of people do, I always say I am the daughter of Nell Mary and Augustus Shealey. Why God blessed me with such beautiful parents, I don't know, but I rejoice.

I was born and raised in Cleveland, Ohio. I've lived many other places, but Cleveland is my home. And I lived in one house my entire life, until I entered the convent.

That house was on East 73rd and Cedar Avenue. Of course, it's changed quite a bit since I was a child. But sometimes, when I'm riding in a car with people driving through the old neighborhood, I look around and I see myself as a child — running down the street, going to the grocery store, visiting a friend, or just crossing the street — like it was yesterday. I never say a word to the other people in the car as we're passing through, but that's what I'm thinking.

Most people my age grew up in a neighborhood. We didn't move as much from place to place as people do now. And our whole neighborhood was like a family. There's an old African saying, "It takes a village to raise a child." Well I lived in a village growing up.

Everybody in our neighborhood knew each other and everybody took care of one another. You knew Mrs. Townsend next door. You knew Mrs. Fuller on the other side. You knew the Cooks down the Street. You knew the Billups and the Billups knew you. You knew them because they were your mothers or your fathers or your aunts and uncles. You knew them because the people who lived on the blocks that comprised your neighborhood were all family — even if you weren't really related. And everybody who was your friend felt special when they came to your house, because your mother and father treated them that way.

I cherish them all now.

However, I've never met a person, male or female, who in my estimation could hold a candle to Nell Mary and Augustus Shealey. Why do I say that? Because I felt so vividly as a child, when I close my eyes and remember, that I was the most beautiful, talented and important person in the world. And I'm sure all my brothers and sisters felt the same way because our mother and father treated us that way. We were all individuals, and they brought us up that way.

I thought I was just gorgeous. Of course, every child is, but every child doesn't feel that way. And because I felt that way, I knew the sky was the limit.

In our home the dining room table was always set. After dinner we would clean up the plates and put away the food, and my mother would always set the table with our most beautiful dishes. They were never on display where you couldn't touch them, and she never told us not to touch them. You knew they were there for you — that they belonged to you as much as anyone else in the family.

We had friends in, but things were seldom broken. When children are afraid to break things, they become so careful, they actually become careless. And our house was always filled with kids.

I remember asking my mother once why I was so happy. And she said, "Because when I knew that you were going to come, I was so happy — and so was your father. We were so happy that you were going to be born."

And I remember, too, how she told me that an expectant mother was sacred and holy because there was new life growing within.

When I was just a teenager, I remember asking my mother, "Mother Darling, what is it that makes you so beautiful? What is it that makes my friends want to be with you when they have their own mothers and fathers?"

And without hesitation, she said, "I love God."

I said, "Well I do, too."

And she said, "I have the Spirit. I have the Holy Ghost."

I said, "Well I want it, too."

And she said, "Ask for it and you will receive it."

All through grade school and even into high school, Mother would

I can see it when I pass through the old neighborhood in a car. I can see it through the flickering, fading shadows of a little girl playing in the neighborhood at East 73rd and Cedar.

always ask me how my day was — and she'd listen. You knew she really meant it. I used to always say, "I can't wait to tell Mother." Even years later, after my mother died, I would still say it. Then I would think, yes, I will tell her, but it won't be the same way. And when I'm tempted to do something my mother wouldn't do because I am angry or annoyed, I stop because I know my mother wouldn't like it.

I remember it so vividly now. I can see it when I'm just sitting in contemplation. I can see it when I pass through the old neighborhood in a car. I can see it through the flickering, fading shadows of a little girl playing in the neighborhood at East 73rd and Cedar. I can see how people responded to Nell Mary and Augustus Shealey.

And I realize I am blessed.

So I had a very good start. I've thought about my upbringing many times — even more as I get older. I grew up in a house where you were always loved, and the people who came into the house were loved, too.

That made a world of difference in the kind of person I am now. It's the kind of upbringing I want for all children.

Sister Juanita Shealey, CSJ, educator and radio personality. Photographed at the Congregation of the Sisters of St. Joseph.

john Adams

remember when you were young, how there were some things in life you were all excited to see, but then when you finally saw them it was a disappointment? Well, Cleveland Municipal Stadium lived up to everything I'd ever heard. I saw my first baseball game when I was only three years old, but to this very day I can still remember walking up the ramp to the field. I went from the gray of downtown's buildings to the vibrant colors of major league baseball. It was like Dorothy opening the door on the Land of Oz.

I lived at 3624 East 103rd Street and my dad and I walked down and caught the Number 15 bus at 103rd and Union. We got off at East 4th and Prospect and I remember walking by what I thought was a store with two pickle barrels as large as I was. Of course, it was Otto Moser's restaurant, but what did I know then. Those pickle barrels would get smaller and smaller as the years went by.

As we walked to the park, everything was gray — the concrete, asphalt and big buildings. We crossed the West 3rd Street bridge into the cavernous tunnel that led inside the stadium. The sights and sounds were magical. I could smell popcorn, hot dogs, candy. Vendors were hawking programs. There was energy in the air.

My dad had tickets close to home plate so we could see everything — it was, after all, my first game. As I walked up that ramp the first thing I saw was that big blue sky, and each step coming up the ramp revealed more and more of a world that before had existed only in my dreams. First there were the seats, then all the people and excitement, and then, when we finally got to the top, that beautiful green field.

I knew even then that I would always love baseball. In more than 30 years, I've probably only missed 18 games.

I got the idea to take a bass drum to the Indians games back in 1973. Actually, I really do play drums. I started in high school, first at St. Ignatius and later at Parma High, where I graduated in 1969. I used to lead cheers for our football team — my bass drum strapped to my chest, a megaphone in one hand, a mallet in the other. I even organized the first pep band for basketball at Parma High. Back then, bands were illegal at basketball games because the gyms were so small. I organized some people who wanted to play and then called and asked if we could play at a game. They said we could as long was we didn't interfere with the game. "If the referee tells you to stop," they said, "then you're outta here."

That's the same thing Dan Zerby, who was head of Cleveland Municipal Stadium operations, told me when I called him before I brought my bass drum to an Indians game for the first time. It was August 24, 1973, and we played Texas. I bought a used drum set for $25, and the bass drum I still use is the one from that set. It really is a junky old drum, but its resonance and sound made it perfect for that old stadium. I guess you'd just have to call it dumb luck.

I made a name for myself banging that old drum out in the bleachers and have many fond memories of Cleveland Municipal Stadium. But my fondest memory, is also my most bittersweet. It was October 3, 1993, the day the Indians played their last game in the old stadium.

We were playing the White Sox that day. I remember going down to the dugout to do an interview. It was more than an hour before the game, and when I finished my interview I started walking out on that old walkway that circled the box seats. One guy stopped me and asked me for my autograph. Then someone else walked up and asked if they could take a picture with me. Before you knew it, there was a lineup of people. Soon, it went all the way down the rail to the bullpen. People started blocking the aisles and pushing, and I told them all that I wasn't going anywhere. And they all politely lined up. I stood there meeting them, answering their questions. I talked to each one. It was a tremendous honor, but it was also very sad.

As the game started, I couldn't get into my usual seats because it wasn't general admission, you had to purchase every seat. Still, I had bought enough tickets for all of my friends who used to come to the games and we sat close enough together — and of course I had my drum there.

When the game was over, people started to leave, but I decided to go back up to my old seats in the middle of the bleachers in the top of Section 55. I needed to be there one last time. So all of us went up there and we just sat and looked out at the old stadium as people filed out.

The ushers and police didn't hurry us... they all walked out ahead of me. I was the last fan to walk out of the bleachers at a baseball game at Cleveland Municipal Stadium.

It was pretty empty, but there were still about 7,000 or 8,000 people just hanging out taking one last look. None of the ushers or police bothered us. It was a beautiful afternoon, a little chilly, and I kept thinking to myself, "One last time." And I just started banging that junky old drum. I didn't realize it at the time, but when I was done — everybody in the place was dead quiet. They were all looking at me. And then there was this big applause from everyone left in the stadium — the fans, the ushers, the police.

When they were finished we walked down to the exit. The ushers and police didn't hurry us. In fact, they all came up to say good-bye. And they gave me what I consider to be one of the biggest honors of my life. They all walked out ahead of me. I was the last fan to walk out of the bleachers at a baseball game at Cleveland Municipal Stadium.

Of course, I'm at the new stadium now. The first year, it was just the hip place to be; there weren't many real baseball fans. But by the second year, the baseball fans were back. I'm still there most games, and I still have my drum. I sit in section 182, Row Y. I'm in seat 29, and my drum is in seat 28.

John Adams, unofficial drummer for the Cleveland Indians. Photographed at Jacobs Field.

joe Eszterhas

I was a geeky little refugee kid who looked like Howdy Doody, and my mother was a desperately shy woman who couldn't speak the English language. Whenever she went shopping at the West Side Market, 16 blocks from our apartment on Lorain Avenue, I went with her as her helper and translator.

I fell in love with the smells of the world at the market — with grilling bratwurst and just-opened sacks of apples and crates of pears and the woodsy bonfires that the vendors lighted up in the alley behind the market to warm their hands. The vendors were gruff, sleepy, chain-smoking men, mostly immigrants themselves, who treated this black-babushkaed Hungarian woman with great respect and kidded her geeky son.

One vendor, a rough-hewn Italian named Vito, tossed me an apple or an orange or a pear every time he saw me. And he saw me a lot because the grade school I went to, St. Emeric's, was only a few hundred feet from the market and I had to pass through the market every day to get there.

Imagine that! All those hundreds of apples and pears through the years, tossed to me with the words "Here ya go, Joey!" underneath a thick Italian accent. I thought about Vito a lot as I grew into a man. Who knows what little things make a little boy love America? I came to the conclusion that Vito played a very large part in the way I grew to love this great country.

Forty years later, in 1993, I took the woman who is the love of my life to the West Side Market for the first time to share my childhood with her. A limo dropped us off nearby and we walked to the market. I saw a group of men eyeing us and the limo. And a very old man among them yelled "Here ya go, Joey!" in a thick Italian accent. And he threw me an orange!

When our oldest was seven, we moved from Malibu, on California's gold coast, back to Cleveland. I think the biggest reason we moved back is so that our four boys could experience the sheer heart-pumping joy of walking through the West Side Market.

It made me cry, of course, and I introduced Vito to the love of my life who, poetically, happens to be part Italian.

I married Naomi Baka (from Mansfield, Ohio) and we had four boys. When our oldest was seven, we moved from Malibu, on California's gold coast, back to Cleveland. I think the biggest reason we moved back is so that our four boys could experience the sheer heart-pumping joy of walking through the West Side Market.

Who knows? Maybe somebody will toss them an apple or a pear or an orange sometime.

The vendors were gruff, sleepy, chain-smoking men, mostly immigrants themselves, who treated this black-babushkaed Hungarian woman with great respect and kidded her geeky son.

Joe Eszterhas, screenwriter and author.
Photographed at his home in Bainbridge.

dick Pogue

my father was a Wall Street lawyer, so from the time I was very young I always wanted to be in the legal profession. I wanted to have a New York-style corporate practice; I just didn't want to live around New York. When Jones Day made me an offer to come to Cleveland in 1957, it seemed to be a nice compromise between what I was looking for professionally and having a halfway decent place to live. Since then, I've always wanted to be here, and I've always enjoyed being in court.

During my years in Cleveland as a lawyer and later as the managing partner of Jones Day, I've been a part of some pretty important and well-publicized cases. The Mobil/Marathon takeover was one such case. Pat McCartan and John Stroud did the court appearances, and I was the strategist working with Joe Flom. Mobil was attempting a hostile takeover of Marathon and we were trying to stop it. It was a very high-profile case at the time, and there was publicity all across the country.

It's funny, but the part of the trial that sticks out most today, aside from the outcome, has very little to do with case itself. We had a hearing here in Cleveland in front of Judge Manos, who ruled his court with an iron fist. The courtroom was absolutely packed. The bailiff had locked the doors so no one else could get in.

When Judge Manos walked into the courtroom, the bailiff called the proceedings to order and there was absolute silence. Several hundred people and there was absolute silence — except two young women reporters in the back row whispering to one another. You could have heard a pin drop, except for their whispering.

Manos heard this and his eyes flew open wide. Everybody else in the courtroom knew what was happening, except these two who were still whispering. Manos stood up with his gavel, pointed at these two women, banged his gavel down so hard I thought it would break, and yelled out, "We will have order in this court!"

I felt sorry for them. I don't ever think I've seen anybody shrink down farther in their seats than these two. They were just mortified.

Mobil was attempting a hostile takeover of Marathon and we were trying to stop it. It was a very high-profile case at the time, and there was publicity all across the country.

We won the day, of course. We got a preliminary injunction against Mobil's raid on Marathon. Eventually, the Marathon board decided to sell out to U.S. Steel. It was a pretty big case at the time, and I was, of course, very happy with the outcome. But I can still see those two women, shrinking down in their seats, wishing more than anything that they could be anyplace else — anyplace other than a courtroom in Cleveland.

It was a pretty big case at the time, and I was, of course, very happy with the outcome. But I can still see those two women, shrinking down in their seats, wishing more than anything that they could be anyplace else—anyplace other than a courtroom in Cleveland.

Richard Pogue, attorney, public relations executive and civic leader.
Photographed in downtown Cleveland.

ron Sweed

as a kid growing up in Euclid, I set four major goals for myself: that one day, I'd work for Ghoulardi; that I'd meet the Beatles, especially John Lennon; that I'd have a television show of my own by the time I was 21; and that I'd make a million dollars.

Thanks to Ernie Anderson, the first three came true. I'm still working on the fourth. I met Mr. Anderson in the summer of 1963 when I was 13 years old — the same year I stole a gorilla suit.

I lived just off East 260th right up the street from the lake. That's where we hung out in summer. We had great beach parties. So right there I had a pretty good start as a kid growing up.

In February of 1963, Mr. Anderson came on the air as Ghoulardi, and right about that same time everyone in the neighborhood became rabid fans. He started out with one show on Friday night at 11:30 after "City Camera News" on Channel 8. Later that summer he added a half-hour show called "Laurel, Ghoulardi and Hardy" from 4:30 to 5 p.m. Then he added another show on Saturday evening called "Ghoulardi's Masterpiece Theater."

On Friday nights, we would all go up the road to either the Shore or Lake theaters on Lake Shore Boulevard. All the girls would be up there and you would just pair off with whoever you wanted to be with that night and supposedly watch the movie. Sometimes there was very little movie watching going on. But we always had to be home at 11:30 to watch Ghoulardi.

That's when I decided I wanted to work for Ghoulardi.

That summer, I went to the Shore Theater with a bunch of friends to see Dr. Zolkini and his Live Stage of Horrors Show. I remember the ads, "See the Frankenstein Monster, King Kong, the Mummy." We figured it would be good for an afternoon of laughs, so a bunch of us went. They showed two or three horror movies and these guys in cheap, cheesy costumes would run across the stage during the movies.

When the show was over, we walked out back to cut through the woods to get back to our neighborhood, but as we did, there was Dr. Zolkini packing up his gear. It was his misfortune to leave a trunk unattended.

I've always been fascinated by gorilla suits. I always liked the Three Stooges stuff with gorillas. When I saw that gorilla suit, I just said, "Hot damn, now's my chance." So as my gang passed by I grabbed it and ran into the woods.

The whole gang gathered around me. I said, "Let me put this bad boy on." I walked the rest of the way home with the gorilla suit on.

As we came out of the woods and started to walk down the street toward our neighborhood, we kept picking up more and more people. "Hey, look at the gorilla," they said. By the time we got to the top of our street, there was a large group of people heading toward our house.

My mom remembers this quite vividly, because she was in the yard that day. She couldn't tell what was going on because I was surrounded.

But she saw there was great interest in the middle of the crowd, and she knew I had to be the cause of it.

Growing up, I was the class clown, and a troublemaker. I was good for a call from school every day or from a neighbor during the summer. So showing up in a gorilla suit wasn't a big surprise. When she saw me, I said, "Hey mom, look at this great gorilla suit." And she said, "So, are they just giving them away at the theater?"

"Well sort of," I said. Eventually I disclosed how I'd come by the suit, and she said, "Oh great, my son the gorilla thief."

As luck would have it Ghoulardi was appearing at Euclid Beach Park the next day. Of course, we had already made plans to be down there to see him. He had a show at 3, then another at 6 and still another at 7:30.

I figured if I wore the gorilla suit, I'd probably catch his attention, maybe get to meet him and get an autograph. So I put on the suit and one of my buddies pilfered his dog's collar and leash so he could be part of the act. We all headed up to Lake Shore Boulevard to catch the bus to Euclid Beach. There must have been five or six of us.

But the bus driver had no sense of humor at all. "Hey, he's gotta take off that gorilla head if he's gonna ride," he said.

I guess he had to go by the rules. No animals allowed. I had to prove I was human by taking off the head.

We got to the park, and I started to walk around on a leash with my buddy. He was the trainer, taming the wild beast. Soon we had a crowd around us, and everybody thought I was Ghoulardi — that Ghoulardi was walking around in a gorilla suit. Of course, we did nothing to dispel the rumor.

At 3 o'clock, Ghoulardi came on. He was on a big stage set up between The Thriller and Laugh in the Dark. It was the same day that Manner's came out with the Big Ghoulardi, some sort of new drink.

But I went back too far and fell off the stage. It was about 6 feet high. The next thing I know I'm on my back like an armadillo with my feet and arms in the air. And I see Ghoulardi peering down at me.

Ghoulardi said, "Ayy group, I wouldn't drink it, but if any of you loyal kniffs out there would like to try it, go ahead."

That's when he spotted me.

"Hey I don't believe it. Ova dey. Look at that gorilla, group. Come up here, baby."

Then he started in on his routine. "Hey, Ghoulardi ain't afraid of no gorilla. Back you beast! Back!"

But I went back too far and fell off the stage. It was about 6 feet high. The next thing I know I'm on my back like an armadillo with my feet and arms in the air. And I see Ghoulardi peering down at me. He said, "You okay, baby?"

The whole suit was heavily padded, so I was fine. So I grunted back

Ron Sweed, The Ghoul.
Photographed on the set of his show.

in gorilla, "Oooh! Oooh! Oooh!"

That broke him up and he started laughing pretty hard. So I got back up on stage with him and we finished the act. After the show, I went back to his dressing room, which was just a small area in the middle of the gears and oil room of Laugh in the Dark.

I got my autographed Ghoulardi postcard, which I still have to this day. I asked if I could come back for the two shows later that day, and he said, "Hey, dat's cool, anything you want."

I went back with my friends and watched "Laurel, Ghoulardi and Hardy" later that afternoon, and sure enough, there I was on stage with Ghoulardi. We took the bus back down for the next two shows later that day, and soon, I became a regular on his Friday night show.

That meeting led to a lot of wonderful things. Because I worked at Channel 8, I was able to meet the Beatles. Ernie gave me an 8 mm movie camera for Christmas, and when the Beatles came to town in 1964, I got a press pass and the cameramen gave me Channel 8 stickers for my 8 mm. I even managed to con my way into their room. They used my 8 mm footage on "City Camera News." They sent me to their concert in Toronto in 1965 when the Beatles were banned by Mayor Locher. I even covered them when they returned in 1966.

When Ghoulardi left town in 1966, I started working for Big Chuck and Houlihan. I went off to college at Bowling Green, but would come back on the weekends to do the show. In 1970, Ernie Anderson came back for a television special, and I tried to talk him into coming back as Ghoulardi. As Ghoulardi he was the most recognizable character on Cleveland television. He was also the highest paid commercial announcer in town. But it was history and he was tired of it.

Then I approached him about my recreating the Ghoulardi character. At first he didn't like the idea. He was very good friends with Big Chuck Schodowski, and I was stepping on his toes. He also thought I was a little too low-key. He finally gave me his blessing. The name Ghoulardi was owned by Storer Broadcasting and I couldn't use it. So Ernie Anderson, or Mr. Anderson as I called him, christened me "The Ghoul."

I landed a four-week trial run at Channel 61, and broke from my dead-on impersonation of Ghoulardi into a more '70s-style show. I had my own show, and I was only 21 years old. The Ghoul has been syndicated in a number of different towns. I make a comfortable living just selling Ghoul memorabilia. And I still do radio and television.

But that was how I got my start — by stealing a gorilla suit and meeting the great Ghoulardi at Euclid Beach Park. He was a comedic genius and like a second father to me. That's why, to this day, I still refer to him as Mr. Anderson. ❧

Growing up, I was the class clown, and a troublemaker. I was good for a call from school every day or from a neighbor during the summer. So showing up in a gorilla suit wasn't a big surprise.

On Friday nights, we would all go up the road to either the Shore or Lake theaters on Lake Shore Boulevard. All the girls would be up there and you would just pair off with whoever you wanted to be with that night and supposedly watch the movie.

jenni Meno

ce skating — when you train at a high level, it takes up all of your time. You just can't fit anything else in. That's why you have to love it. You have to make sacrifices. So do the people around you.

Now that I'm older and look back, I'm happy I was able to go to Westlake High School because I had a normal high school, even though I was in training. I had friends and did normal things like go to football games. Skating and school were two separate things for me, which I think was really good for me.

I still call Westlake home, even though I don't live there anymore. My parents still do. The people just seem more friendly there, more down-to-earth. The whole town and all my friends were very supportive of skating when I was there.

I got my first taste of skating when I was five. We lived in Chicago back then. My mother is the second oldest of 11 children, so her two youngest sisters are only a few years older than I am. They were into skating, so naturally I wanted to skate, too. My mom took me skating with them. We did our first little ice show together. Then one of my uncles gave me a pair of skates for Christmas. That's how I got interested.

But I did the bulk of my skating in Ohio. A few years after I got interested in skating, my family moved to Columbus. When I was 10, I was at the point where I needed to move on to a better coach. All the rinks in Columbus were closing down, so my parents looked around for a new place to skate.

Skating is a small world, so you hear about everyone and everything. My parents heard about a place in Lakewood called Winterhurst. The coach there was Carol Heiss Jenkins, the 1960 Olympic champion.

When my parents first met Carol, they really liked her, not just because of her skating background, but because of the person she was. They knew I would be spending a lot of time with her and I needed a good role model growing up.

So I started training at Winterhurst. At first it was very difficult for my family and me. I have three younger brothers and my parents wanted our family to be together. But they also knew how much I loved skating, so they were willing to make the sacrifice.

My grandfather would drive me up to Winterhurst early Monday morning. We'd start out at 5 a.m. and be on the ice by 7:30. I slept most of the way. Then, I'd be in Lakewood all week, staying with another family and going to school there. But I'd always go back to Columbus on Friday night.

When my grandfather passed away, my grandmother moved to Lakewood and I stayed with her during the week, which was better, but still not good. That's when my parents' business changed and they were able to move up to Cleveland.

My parents eventually settled in Westlake, and really wanted me to go to school there. A lot of times, schools aren't all that understanding about your need to train. They went and talked to the school officials in Westlake, and the school made an arrangement where I would complete my classes before 12:30 and then have the rest of the day to train. I can't begin to tell you what that meant to me, and what it's meant for my career on ice. They were just so flexible and understanding.

When I wanted to skate pairs, Carol recommended I contact a man in southern California named John Nicks. So I flew out to California with my mom. My initial partner was Scott Wendland, but the first person I met when I flew in was Todd Sand. He was a friend of Scott's. It turns out Scott was working and couldn't make it to the airport, so he asked Todd to come out and pick us up.

I skated with Scott for two years, but Todd and I trained in the same rink, with the same coach. We all competed in the Olympics in 1992, but Todd and I were finished competing on the third day of the Olympics. So we spent a lot of time just hanging out and our relationship just sort of changed from friendship to more romantic.

When the season was over, he decided he wasn't going to skate with his partner, so we started skating together. We both said, "If we're going to be skating together, we're not going to date or anything. It will be a professional skating relationship."

That lasted about a week. Now here we are, married over nine years and expecting our first child.

> **We both said, "If we're going to be skating together, we're not going to date or anything. It will be a professional skating relationship." That lasted about a week. Now here we are, married over nine years and expecting our first child.**

In 1994, my entire family — my three brothers and my parents — got to go to Lillihammer to watch me compete in the Olympics. That was really nice, a sort of thanks for making the sacrifices with me that helped my career.

But I have Westlake to thank as well. All my friends there, all the people who encouraged me to succeed. I still go back there to visit family and friends, but no matter how long I stay, it never seems long enough. There is always someone else to see or something else to do.

The people in Westlake are the greatest people in all the world. That's why Westlake will always be my home. ➳

*Jenni Meno and Todd Sand, three-time Olympic pairs skaters.
Photographed in Laguna Beach, California.*

rev. otis Moss, jr.

People always ask me about my accomplishments. Certainly, I consider the Otis Moss Jr. University Hospitals Medical Center as a breakthrough accomplishment. But one has to be careful about listing one's accomplishments because accomplishments are always based upon those who have gone before you, those who have laid the foundation and those who work with you.

Anything I list as an accomplishment is an expression of my appreciation to the God I serve and the people who have gone before me. I have been blessed with their legacy, and by the people who work with me daily and give me their confidence and support. Of course, my greatest accomplishment has been my daily ministry at Olivet Institutional Baptist Church, which is a 24-hour-a-day calling, touching the lives of individuals on a daily basis in ways that will never be published.

I love Cleveland. I think it's still a town of great potential and promise. But when I came here in 1975, the city was in intensive care, facing tough economic times, unemployment constantly rising. We were in the early stages of the transition away from manufacturing and on the cusp of a shift in the steel industry.

In those days, Republic Steel employed about 15,000 people. We could see what some of the changes were going to be, but they came in rapid fashion. There were families and individuals in our church who worked in the steel mills and earned enough to buy homes, educate their children, have comprehensive medical care and a decent retirement.

But that economy is gone.

In its demise, there is left an incalculable amount of human agony. And our nation has been derelict or negligent in its response. For that reason, we have sought to encourage and support those public officials who have vision and sensitivity. Who are concerned with the needs of the people, in areas of employment, a decent livable wage, and decent medical care and coverage. As well as those who seek opportunities for the education of our children and adults, so they can compete in this highly competitive and globalized world.

We've seen Cleveland go from those high unemployment days of the '70s, the changing economy of the '80s and the years of hope in the '90s. Now we're back again in a terrible economic depression.

But our national leadership has shown no vision or sensitivity to meeting this particular crisis. Hopefully, we will soon get some changes.

I think that has to be the continuing message of the Church. The Gospel of Jesus Christ has to remain a gospel of liberation and a gospel of reconciliation. To me, that's what the whole civil rights movement, as led by Dr. Martin Luther King Jr., was all about: liberation and reconciliation.

I love Cleveland. I think it's still a town of great potential and promise. But when I came here in 1975, the city was in intensive care, facing tough economic times, unemployment constantly rising.

Unfortunately, it's the kind of thing that government is seldom willing to challenge people to do. And yet when they do, they discover again and again that the more secure people are at the bottom, the better it is for those at the top.

There is enough wealth in the world for everybody. But it might mean the wealthy might grow richer at a little slower pace.

With all of its challenges, Cleveland is still a city running over with potential. It hasn't yet begun to dig deep into what it can become, with the lake, the river and its wonderful activist heritage. And that's why I love Cleveland. ☞

In those days, Republic Steel employed about 15,000 people. We could see what some of the changes were going to be, but they came in rapid fashion.

Rev. Dr. Otis Moss Jr., Pastor of the Olivet Institutional Baptist Church. Photographed at his ministry.

jack Riley

got my start in radio in Cleveland when I was 18 years old, but my fascination with radio started well before that. I grew up in Lakewood, the oldest of four boys, and I used to set up a cheese grater on the kitchen table like it was a microphone, play my 45s on a record player and pretend to be a radio disc jockey. My play list included Billy May, Woody Herman and Stan Kenton.

Back then, Cleveland had some terrific radio. Those were the days of Alan Freed, Bill Randle, Phil McClain, Tom Brown and Joe Mulvehill. It set the standard for the rest of the nation. Cleveland radio stations would literally make or break an artist — and I'm talking about people like Elvis Presley — the standard was just that high. At any rate, after my stint at the kitchen table — which doesn't go on my résumé — I worked at the KYW record library while I went to night school at John Carroll University. That's where I met Big Wilson. He had a morning show from 6 to 10 a.m., and then did a thing called "Six O'clock Adventure" on television at night where he'd play

episodes of "Sheena, Queen of the Jungle" — things like that. Then he was back on at 11:20 at night for a 10-minute television show that ran between the news at night and what was then the "Jack Parr Show." Cleveland couldn't get enough of the guy.

Biggy was a jolly, Willard Scott kind of guy, with a lot of soul and a dry sense of humor. And he was big — I mean 6 foot 6, 300 pounds. People used to come up to him and say, "Boy, you really are big. You look so much smaller on TV," and he'd always say, "Well, you probably have a small set." I had a lot of fun working for Big; unfortunately, he is no longer with us. In the late '50s I started running his record hops. We would go out to different schools on the weekends and they would have a dance where we played records. We went all over the area, even out to Canton and Massillon. It was a three-hour show, and we'd always throw in a couple of comedy routines, vaudeville-style. Sometimes we'd even bring along a recording star, people like Frankie Avalon, Johnny Ray or Paul Anka.

Those were the days of Alan Freed, Bill Randle, Phil McClain, Tom Brown and Joe Mulvehill. It set the standard for the rest of the nation. Cleveland radio stations would literally make or break an artist — and I'm talking about people like Elvis Presley — the standard was just that high.

So we'd drive out to these places and put on a show. I used to help set up our little sound system and all our records of Top 40 hits. One time, on a snowy night, we drove all the way down to Akron and Biggy looked at me and said, "Okay let's set up." I told him I couldn't, and he asked me why, and I said, "Because the records are still in your driveway."

So I had to turn around and drive all the way back to Rocky River to get the records. Luckily, Big was also a great piano player, so he just filled in and entertained the crowd for an hour and a half while I drove back to get the records.

I was drafted into the Army in 1958, and about the same time, Tim Conway was just getting out of the service. I came home on furlough in December of that year and we all did a show with Biggy. Tim did his one-man-band routine, and with that show Conway became a lifelong friend.

As you might have guessed, it was a lot of fun when we weren't

working, as well. Biggy had a motorboat, I guess it slept four, and we used to take it out and bring along people from the station. Let me tell you, there was some drinking involved. We used to water ski, I mean I couldn't even swim, and here I was water skiing with nothing on but trunks and a cork-vest lifesaver. Sometimes I'd let go and I'd be bobbing out there for three or four minutes before Big could crank it around to come back to pick me up. Stupid and lucky at the same time. And I lived.

Those were the halcyon days of radio in Cleveland, and I still look back on them and smile to this day. It's one of the reasons I still call Cleveland home. And of course, I still have many friends there, Linn Sheldon and Bill Gordon just to name two. And of course, my partner Jeff Baxter with whom I did "The Baxter & Riley Show" on WERE for five years. He does the best impression of Bill Randle I've ever heard. We were inducted into the Ohio Broadcasters Hall of Fame a couple of years ago.

Thanks, Cleveland.

Jack Riley, actor, radio personality and character voice.
Photographed at Klasky-Csupo, home of the Rugrats.

brian Sipe

liked Cleveland from the first time I saw it. Which is a little strange since it was in pretty rough condition back then. It was late February 1972, I was the recent 13th round draft choice for the Cleveland Browns, and my plane was late arriving from San Diego for our first mini-camp. By the time I landed, the other draftees had already gone out to Case Western Reserve for the workout. The Browns' Gordie Helms stayed behind and as he drove us up I-71, I got my first look at my new home. Until that time, Cleveland was one of those places I'd have had a hard time finding on a map.

I was born and raised in Southern California and was comfortable with the lifestyle — living at the beach, surfing every morning, and not making any plans for a pro football career. The only reasonable post-college plan I had was to wait tables in Steamboat Springs, Colorado, ski, and enjoy the mountain life for awhile. This date to compete at a pro football camp seemed more an adventure than an opportunity. My chances looked a bit slim.

Cleveland didn't put on its best face for me during that drive. So many factories were closed down, and the Cuyahoga River had caught fire the year before. It was a gloomy afternoon, and because it hadn't snowed in a while, what snow remained was dirty. I remember thinking that this was as close as I was ever going to get to the Soviet Union — at least I imagined it that way. By the time we got to Case Western Reserve, the rookie workout was over. The players were showering, Gordie had to leave, and I was left to stand in this cold, gray place waiting for the bus that would take us back to our rooms at the Hollenden House Hotel. Not a good start!

As I waited and worried about my missed opportunity to impress the coaches, an older gentleman approached me. He looked like a cartoon character but with a big smile. He introduced himself as Lou Groza. Now this was ironic because he was the only man in football that my dad had ever mentioned to me. They shared a class together at Ohio State after my dad got out of the Marines. And now here I was with Lou Groza offering to give me a lift back to the hotel, which I gladly accepted.

Lou made me feel welcome. If ever there was a guy that epitomized Cleveland it was Lou. From that day forward, he treated me with dignity and friendship. It was unearned, unexpected, and genuine. On that dark, cold, gray February day, Lou Groza put a smile on the city for me, and suddenly it felt like a much warmer place.

I was less than spectacular my first couple of years. As a 13th rounder, you don't count on a long career and I was happy to survive as the third-string quarterback in 1972 behind Mike Phipps and Bill Nelson. The third QB was always on the Taxi squad back then because they could only suit up 40 players on Sunday. I practiced and traveled with the team, wore sweats and manned a clipboard on the sidelines during the games.

My first home was in Lakewood on Edwards Street in a third-floor attic apartment. It was a great adventure. Cleveland was different from anything I had ever seen. The whole year was surreal to me. I hadn't married my sweetheart Jeri yet, so I partied and had too much fun. As a result, the Browns were not all that impressed and sent me a loud and clear message.

During the next off-season, with two 2nd round draft choices in hand and the retirement of Bill Nelson, the Browns went after two new QBs. My days were numbered. They acquired veteran Don Horn from Denver and used the other second choice on a record setter from Toledo. Phipps was entrenched as their starter, and my place was out the door.

My salvation came on the first day of camp when we were required to bench press 135 pounds as many time as possible. Knowing that my spot was up for grabs during the off season, I had worked hard in the gym and surprised the coaches. Our new 2nd rounder couldn't get the bar off his chest and inadvertently opened a crack in the door that I barged threw to win my spot back.

Still, I sat another year on-the-bench behind Phipps and Horn. The next year, however, they traded Don, moved me up, and gave me a chance to start a game after an off-the-bench come-from behind victory against the Broncos the week before. Ironically, it was against my hometown Chargers in the same stadium that I played in as a San Diego State Aztec. We had averaged only 16 points in our first seven games and the start was partly out of Coach Nick Skorich's frustration over our lack of scoring. It was a great game with a prophetic finish. We scored plenty of points but it came down to one last drive and a chance to kick a field goal to win it. After moving the ball down to the 14-yard line, Coach Skorich decided that I should take a knee closer to the middle of the field to help out our place kicker and run the remaining time off the clock. Then the unthinkable happened. I lost the snap from our center and the Chargers fell on it. We lost 35 to 36. It was 1974.

Of course, everyone knows what happened that cold, gray January day when I drove the Browns down the field against the Raiders to put us in position for one last chance at a playoff-winning field goal.

The next year, I shared some of the playing time with Mike but it was hard for them to give up on him after selecting him with the second overall pick in the 1970 draft. He was a big strong guy who made me look anemic by comparison. In 1976, after playing my heart out in the preseason, they once again chose to start Phipps in our opener against the 49ers. In the very first series, Mike went down hard with a separated shoulder and would miss the next two games. He never saw the field again. We went 9-5 and Mike was traded to the Bears after the season was over.

I've been lucky to be called a tough player by people I respect and I value that. But in good part my toughness was a result of not wanting anyone to do to me what I did to Mike Phipps. It would take something very serious to get me off the field. There were plenty of guys out there who were better that me. But if they couldn't get on

Brian Sipe, former Cleveland Browns quarterback.
Photographed with the senior members of his state champion
Santa Fe Christian High School football team.

brian Sipe

the field, no one would know.

The '78 season ended with a lot of promise and in '79 we opened 3-0 and were scheduled to play the Cowboys at home on Monday night. The town was electric! After being snubbed by national television for much of the '70s, Cleveland would have the Monday Night spotlight for the first time since the innaugral telecast of "Monday Night Football" back in 1970. The Cowboys were undefeated as well and all eyes were on the lakefront.

I've looked back on many memorable games during my 12 years with the Browns but this was special, in good part because my terminally ill father was having a final week of good health and was able to fly back for one last chance to see his son play. Coach Sam Rutigliano and owner Art Modell treated him like royalty. He was allowed past security to watch me practice and enjoy professional football from the inside out. It had been hard for him to see much of my career up close from his home in Hawaii. Now he would see Municipal Stadium packed and rockin' for the biggest game in years. Dad saw me throw three touchdowns in the first half and we never looked back. I loved that old stadium. It was a perfect reflection of the town and a perfect place for the Kardiac Kids to play.

Most of my career was spent as the underdog. The AFC Central was murder. It was that way for all of us, all of the Kardiac Kids. We weren't loaded with talent. We didn't send a lot of guys to the Pro Bowl. But no one wanted to play us. The town identified with that and loved us for it. The enthusiasm, love, and appreciation that we got from everybody, not just the football fans, blew me away.

Of course, everyone knows what happened that cold, gray January day when I drove the Browns down the field against the Raiders to put us in position for one last chance at a playoff-winning field goal.

That was the day I broke Cleveland's heart. A New York reporter approached me only weeks later while I was there to pick up the league's Most Valuable Player Trophy. He told me that the memory would somehow bring the town closer together — that through the shared experience, not only Browns fans but all Clevelanders would become closer. I think he was prophetic.

Most of my career was spent as the underdog. The AFC Central was murder. It was that way for all of us, all of the Kardiac Kids. We weren't loaded with talent. We didn't send a lot of guys to the Pro Bowl.

On that dark, cold, gray February day, Lou Groza put a smile on the city for me, and suddenly it felt like a much warmer place.

herb Score

I consider myself a very lucky man, even though I've faced a great deal of adversity throughout my life. I have no secrets on how to handle adversity. I am just fortunate to be able to accept things for what they are, the way they are, and the way they happen. As I look back, I wouldn't change one thing. I am grateful for the life I have had.

As a player, I can't really think of any one game that stands out. I tried to make every game I pitched my best game. Being named the Indians' first Rookie of the Year in 1955 was, of course, a great honor.

Many people think that Gil McDougald's line shot ended my playing career, but it was really an injury to my throwing arm that happened against the Senators in April of 1958. Of course, the eye injury most likely contributed to my arm injury because of all the cortisone I was taking to keep my retina from detaching. I suppose I could have hurt my arm at some other time without getting hit in the eye with that line shot off McDougald's bat. When I couldn't pitch anymore, I just happened to be in the right place at the right time, and that's how I became a broadcaster. And I am very happy I did become a broadcaster.

After more than 34 years in the broadcast booth for the Indians, my retirement was perhaps my fondest memory. I was overwhelmed by the fans, and the good wishes, and how good the Indians were to me. They surprised me with a retirement ring. It's something I'll always cherish — a memento of my many good days with the Indians and Cleveland.

The Indians organization is still very good to me.

As far as announcing a game is concerned, a standout would have to be May 15, 1981 — Lenny Barker's perfect game. Many people say they were there, but there were only a few thousand people in the stands. The air was thick but cold — with a hint of drizzle and always the threat of rain. Lenny was just on that night. No one could touch him. Some of his pitches were hitting in the dirt in front of the plate, and the batters were still swinging at them. On that last pop up to Rick Manning in center, I think everybody in old Municipal Stadium took a collective breath. But the catch was made and the celebration was on. I can only imagine how many fans had tickets for the game and didn't show up because the weather was bad. It just goes to show you that on any given night you can see history at the ballpark.

Many people think that Gil McDougald's line shot ended my playing career, but it was really an injury to my throwing arm that happened against the Senators in April of 1958.

Naturally, I have many fond memories of Cleveland Municipal Stadium, but I also fell in love with Jacobs Field. The Indians have already built a tradition of success in their new home. It's new, exciting and has all the modern conveniences. Jacobs Field is also building a whole new set of memories for young fans who are sure to be in the stands for years to come.

I can only imagine how many fans had tickets for the game and didn't show up because the weather was bad. It just goes to show you that on any given night you can see history at the ballpark.

Herb Score, former pitching ace and voice of the Cleveland Indians. Photographed at his home in Lakewood.

dr. elizabeth k. Balraj

ver since I was little I wanted to be a physician, and I worked toward that goal growing up in India.

Being a coroner is, of course, a very responsible position. It touches the lives of so many people. I don't think I could talk about any specific case, either seeing something or solving a case. I see a lot of tragedy in my work. And that is a very personal thing.

It may sound funny, but I truly believe that I have the opportunity to help people as coroner. A lot of people can't understand how. Obviously, I can't bring somebody back to life. But at least I can do a thorough investigation and help bring law and justice to the community. I also hope I bring some closure to the families. Like I said, there is a lot of tragedy in my work. And tragedy is a very personal thing.

You might suspect that it might be hard emotionally. It is, but it's also my way of giving back to a community that has given so much to me.

I was born in the south of India in a city called Salem, but I've lived all over India. My father was in the Indian Navy, so we were transferred around quite a bit. I've lived in Bombay and Delhi, and studied medicine at Christian Medical College in a city called Vellore. I have seen quite a few towns in my time. But this one is my home.

I followed my husband here from India. Back then, in India, it was customary to have marriages arranged and that's how I became married to my husband. After being in the USA for seven years and after graduating from college with a degree in engineering, he came back to India and married me. He grew to love the United States, and wanted to make this his home. I love India, but when he came here, I decided to follow my husband.

We first lived in Akron, where I started to specialize in forensic pathology. I was there two years, when both my husband and I decided to move to Cleveland because there were more opportunities. I was in residency at St. Luke's Hospital and we rented a house on Hulda Avenue just across from the hospital — so it was very convenient.

I've lived in Bombay and Delhi, and studied medicine at Christian Medical College in a city called Vellore. I have seen quite a few towns in my time. But this one is my home.

Then I specialized in forensic pathology at the Cuyahoga County Coroner's office. As I grew into my career in forensic pathology, I also grew to love Cleveland because of the very diverse ethnic cultures here. There is an Indian community, but there are also Philippine, Thai and Chinese communities. And it's not just the Asian/Indian communities, but all ethnic communities — German, Irish and Italian — so many different kinds of people. What amazes me most is that even though they come from very diverse backgrounds, they have all embraced me — even though I come from India. Now I do my best every day, in what can be a very difficult job, helping people in times of tragedy, reaching out to the many people in our community.

I guess we all seem to have the same thing in common — Cleveland is our home and, like me, for many people there is no place else they would rather be. And that is truly a very personal thing.

Being a coroner is, of course, a very responsible position. It touches the lives of so many people. I don't think I could talk about any specific case, either seeing something or solving a case. I see a lot of tragedy in my work. And that is a very personal thing.

Elizabeth K. Balraj, M.D., Cuyahoga County Coroner.
Photographed in the autopsy room.

daffy dan Gray

t was 1973 and I was running a chain of record stores under names like Melody Lane, Music Grotto, and Pearl Alley Discs when a light bulb went off. That's the way it's been ever since I was a kid when I get great ideas. Every project I've ever done has begun with a light bulb turning on in my head.

This light bulb was T-shirts, and that's how Daffy Dan's began. It's hard to comprehend now, but in 1973 putting words and pictures on the clothes you wore was something of a novel idea. I wasn't the first person to start printing T-shirts — probably not even the first in Cleveland — but I brought to it the marketing I learned from the record stores and by listening to my mentor Larry Robinson, The Diamond Man. We began Daffy Dan's with just one store on Cleveland's West Side and grew to 27 stores in just six years.

I think the 1970s was a golden time to do what I did. Everything was just right for Daffy Dan's to succeed. The rock 'n' roll scene here was great. WMMS was the best radio station in the country and needed both a source for tens of thousands of T-shirts for their listeners and outlets where they could be sold. T-shirts were becoming the in thing. That's what we wore in those days, T-shirts and Levis, and we still do! Everyone thought it was a fad. Some fad. And of course, everyone wanted the signature Double Ds on their sleeves, because "If your T-shirt doesn't have a Double D on the sleeve… it's just UNDERWEAR!!" Without a doubt, I couldn't have picked a better time or place to start Daffy Dan's.

I love Cleveland. I always have. I've been fascinated with Cleveland for as long as I can remember. What a great city! When I was a kid, it was a blue-collar town where people worked hard and played hard. In the '70s you saw a lot of that energy in the music and club scene. I think my shirts gave people a chance to express themselves. They became walking billboards. One of my advertising slogans was, "We'll print it, if you'll wear it!!"

Clevelanders were getting tired of being the butt of jokes on late-night TV. Remember all the wisecracks about the burning river and the Parma jokes? Well, that's not who we were. We knew it, and we wanted to tell people. The T-shirt gave all of us the opportunity to express ourselves and be who we wanted to be.

Daffy Dan's was a mixture of hard work and creativity. But even more, it was being in the right place at the right time, and the right place was Cleveland. I don't think I could have done what I did anyplace else.

What I still can't believe is the warm response I've had from the people of Cleveland. I'm just this guy who sells T-shirts and loves rock 'n' roll, but when I walk the streets of this town you'd think I was somebody important. I get recognized everywhere. Sure, I look a little different from most people. I still have the long hair that got me thrown out of Shaker High in 1968, and I've worn the same sideburns and moustache for better than 30 years. I'm sure the fact that the Daffy Dan's logo is a cartoon of me helps, but the fact is people recognize me.

What really makes me feel good, though, is that they all want to tell me a story about a shirt they got way back when, or a time when they hung out with me at some music club. I've always wanted people to have a good time with my products, and it's so much fun when they tell me these stories. For a couple of generations of Clevelanders, getting that first T-shirt from Daffy Dan's that said what they wanted it to say has been something like a rite of passage. I love that, but I'm still surprised by how people relate to me personally!

I wasn't the first person to start printing T-shirts — probably not even the first in Cleveland — but I brought to it the marketing I learned from the record stores and by listening to my mentor Larry Robinson, The Diamond Man.

I remember one time in the late 1980s when I was hanging out with some friends at the old Sweetwater at Huron and East 14th. The servers were getting together to sing Happy Birthday to a girl who was turning 14. She was at a nearby table with her parents. One of my friends suggested we join them in the singing, so we did. Later the girl's father came over and asked me for my autograph for his daughter. He told me she said that it was the best birthday of her life because Daffy Dan sang Happy Birthday to her.

I mean if that doesn't make you feel good, what does?

Another time, I'm walking down this street with my buddy Dave in a little mountain town in North Carolina and a car rolls by. It turns around and comes back real slow. A guy hangs out the window and shouts "Hey, Daffy Dan!" I've had people shout that at me in Europe and even as far away as Australia.

It sure is nice to be recognized like that, but you know, it's really not about me. It's about Cleveland. When they shout, "Hey, Daffy Dan!" they're really saying, "Hey, I'm from Cleveland." And that's great, because so am I! ➤

I don't think I could have done what I did anyplace else.

Daffy Dan Gray, founder, grand poobah and chairman emeritus of Daffy Dan T-shirts. Photographed on the Veterans Memorial Bridge with his dog, Smedley.

fred Griffith

Cleveland was the first big city I ever saw. I think it was in 1948. As a college student, I lived in West Virginia in a sliver of a town that occupied the valley of a small river and some of the runs and draws and hollows nearby. My hometown of Charleston wasn't much bigger.

A college friend who owned an old car wanted to come to Cleveland to apply for graduate studies at Western Reserve. He invited us to make the drive with him. It was an all-day journey back then; no interstates, and even the smallest little town had at least one stoplight. When we got to what they called University Circle we squeezed into the small off-campus apartment of one of his friends. We drank a beer or two at the nearby bar. And we scored standing room tickets at Severance Hall to hear George Szell conduct the Cleveland Orchestra.

Later that year I went to Pittsburgh for the first time and we hitchhiked to New York. But it was Cleveland that caught me. Cleveland was a really big city back then, perhaps the nation's seventh largest. The suburban sprawl had not yet started and there were nearly a million people living within its boundaries.

That was at a time when the heavy industry on which our economy was based was hot. Thousands of people were drawn to Cleveland for the good-paying industrial jobs. And in my West Virginia at that time, there was a joke that the three r's were readin', ritin' and Route 21.

After college I did radio news in Charleston for several years. But I knew that for economic reasons I needed to move to a larger city. Cleveland, because of that wonderful first visit, was my choice. It was a place where I had friends, it was a city I knew (at least better than the others), and it had a lively broadcast community.

I got my job here in the fall of 1959, reading the news on a station that played a lot of classical music. It turns out that my having come to Severance Hall a decade earlier had something to do with my being hired.

We rented a wonderful old house in Lakewood. (I think it was built in 1912.) Then when we saved up some money we bought one. We had wonderful neighbors there, including Bill Wambsganss, the only man who ever made an unassisted triple play in a World Series game. Our kids went to Lakewood's good schools. Every morning I drove the Shoreway downtown where our radio station occupied the fourth floor of a solid old building at 1515 Euclid. It was long enough ago that there was a real person who ran the elevator and knew every one who worked in the building.

Playhouse Square was alive back then. The famous Colonnade Cafeteria was in the lower level of our building and hundreds of people crammed into it every day. There were famous restaurants and bars all over the place. The big downtown movie theaters were still alive. And stage shows came to town regularly.

It was the golden age of downtown shopping.

The Sterling Lindner Davis department store was just a couple of blocks up the street. And all through the 1960s, I would take the kids there to see the big Christmas tree that filled the lobby of that wonderful store. Halle's, with Mr. Jingaling, was just across the street. Higbee's was down Euclid at Public Square. They were always trying to outdo each other with spectacular holiday window displays that would grab and hold the children until their parents agreed to take them inside.

In the '60s and '70s, my son, Wally, would say, "Let's get lost." And we would. We would get into the car and take long Sunday drives in the city.

In the '60s and '70s, my son, Wally, would say, "Let's get lost." And we would. We would get into the car and take long Sunday drives in the city. We would head off in some direction and along streets that we had not explored before. Eventually we got to see every wonderful ethnic neighborhood in the region. And we would always find an open bakery where we would experience the diverse food traditions of the people who kept Cleveland working.

As a radio, and later a television, reporter, I covered the daily happenings; but back then, very few of us anticipated the economic decline that was coming or the challenges it would present us. But all of my experiences with that earlier Cleveland and its warm and creative people have kept me optimistic. I am fueled by my warm memories of those wonderful early years. I will always be confident that we will make it. ☞

But it was Cleveland that caught me. Cleveland was a really big city back then, perhaps the nation's seventh largest.

*Fred Griffith, television personality.
Photographed at WKYC-TV.*

arsenio Hall

t's weird how the best stuff that works in stand-up and on television comes from reality. I pulled a lot of my characters from people I used to know in Cleveland, like the barber I played in "Coming to America." He was the character who couldn't cut hair but just ate all day. I stole that guy from a man named Troy who worked for the guy who used to cut my hair when I was little.

Dawson's Barbershop was on Holton Street, a block away from my dad's church, the Elizabeth Baptist Church. My dad was always at the church at choir rehearsal or studying, so it was really easy for me to walk from the church and grab a haircut.

But when you came into the barbershop, the first thing you noticed was that Troy never had any customers. He would just be sitting there with a bag of some food he brought from home, and he would always say, "I'm available, anyone want a haircut?" And everybody would just say, "No thanks, I'll wait for Mr. Dawson."

The Baptist minister I played in the movie is half my father and half a pastor from Chicago named Reverend Humphrey who was a friend of my father's. I took the rhythm from my dad, but most of the dialogue came from this other Reverend. I used to always joke that he could take one word and preach for an hour. And one of the examples would be the word joy:

"I got joy in my heart!
I got joy in my soul!
'J' It stands for Jesus!
'O' It stands for overjoyed!"

And he'd go on and on like that, but the rhythm, that deep inhaling in and out and catching his breath, and then another run-on sentence — that was definitely my father.

Even though there was a podium and pulpit at the Elizabeth Baptist Church, he would always pull the microphone out of its holder and start down the steps into the congregation and up the aisle — but the reason it was so complicated was we didn't have wireless mikes back then.

So the wire was all over the place and it was a chore keeping up with him. There was actually a deacon who worked like a grip to keep my dad from getting hung up on some lady's leg. I mean the last thing you want to do is sweep some 60-year old lady's leg. I mean:

"Ooh, you got my leg! Ahhhhhh!"

That's why I specifically asked Jon Landis to use a microphone with a cord in the movie, because it created that whole ability to remember how my dad did it. Sometimes those little vehicles like that, a cord, will force you to imitate movement and the things that remind you of his style.

I have a lot of fond memories of growing up in Cleveland. But growing up where I did, my first idols were (and it's strange how the range and longitude is in that kind of thing) the pimps and numbers runners. As a kid my uncle ran numbers and one of his friends was Don King. If you lived on the streets of Cleveland in that area, you knew all the pimps and numbers runners.

The first time I ever saw a Rolls Royce, Don King was in it. It was at Public Auditorium for some fight. This was after he went away and came back. But before that, I knew him as an associate of my uncle. And you looked up to those guys because they had nice cars. I didn't know any black doctors, and I only knew one black lawyer, so my role models were somewhat limited. But then I turned on television and there was Flip Wilson and Johnny Carson.

I wanted to do what Johnny did, but when I watched Flip there became an awareness that I could do it, because I am watching this man in prime time and that shows me that even though there is no black late-night talk show host, there can be by the time I'm a man. So that stuff was important to me, because I didn't want to be Jimmy Walker, for obvious reasons.

I graduated from Warrensville Heights High School, but I started at Kennedy in the Lee-Harvard area. My mom thought I was getting in too much trouble in tenth grade. That's when I discovered women and cars, and that became my life. So my mother tried to get me away from certain friends. I understand now that she was trying to get my grade point average up so I could go to college. I'll be honest with you, at that point I was talkin' stuff like, "I don't need no school because I'm gonna be an entertainer or a pimp."

It's a hard thing for a mother to explain to you that there are no dental benefits in pimping. And she explained it to me with a wooden spoon in her hand. When you're bigger than your mom, a wooden spoon is necessary. She would say, "There are no dental benefits in bein' a pimp, what kind of retirement plan do you think they have!" All the time hittin' me in the shoulder blade with the spoon.

A lot of people don't believe in spanking a child, but when he's bigger than you and this is your last shot of keeping him out of jail

As a kid my uncle ran numbers and one of his friends was Don King. If you lived on the streets of Cleveland in that area, you knew all the pimps and numbers runners.

down in Chillicothe — let's just say my mother and father were determined to get it right. And I thank them for every stroke of that spoon because they kept me where I needed to be.

I went to Ohio University in Athens, and then later to Kent State, where I got my degree. That's where I saw a guy by the name of Franklin Ajaye doing stand-up. He was promoting a movie called "Car Wash." That's when I decided to get into stand-up. From there I went to Chicago where I met Nancy Wilson, then out to L.A. where Jay Leno helped me get an apartment and a motorcycle in the same day — that was the strangest day of my life. It's also where I met Eddie Murphy. But, as they say, that's another whole story.

CAUTION
DO N
WHEN

STA

Arsenio Hall, comedian and actor.
Photographed at Hollywood Center Studios,
Hollywood, California.

william Preucil

or me, the big attraction for moving to Cleveland was The Cleveland Orchestra. But when I discovered everything else the city has to offer, I was pleasantly surprised.

I moved here in 1995 after auditioning for concertmaster in 1994. At the time, I was teaching at the Eastman School in Rochester, New York, but I couldn't come here for a year due to previous concert commitments. The year before I came here was spent in anticipation.

I really didn't know what to expect. Of course, The Cleveland Orchestra has a reputation as one of the premier orchestras in the world. I had also studied violin at Indiana University with Josef Gingold, a former concertmaster of The Cleveland Orchestra. I heard, from him, many stories of his days with the orchestra. So I knew about The Cleveland Orchestra long before I came here.

I was already an established concert musician, so I wasn't as anxious about performing as much as I was about coming to the city itself. I had performed here before. My sister went to school here, and I used to visit her. So I was somewhat familiar with the city, but I really didn't know it. And I also had some experiences with other cities during my career that were, well, let's just say there were some places I lived where it never felt like home.

My family lived in one city for seven years, and we never got used to it. Sometimes, when I was on the road performing, I would tell someone I was going home and then tell them the wrong town. That has never happened here.

So I had a year to wonder whether coming to Cleveland was a good move. I knew it was the right decision the very first day I appeared on stage at Severance Hall as a member of the orchestra.

It was mid-April of 1995. The spring was beautiful that year. We started rehearsing on Tuesday for a concert on Thursday. When I walked on stage that evening, the reception from both my colleagues and the audience was so warm, it was indescribable. It gave me the immediate feeling the move was right. It didn't take long before my family settled in and Cleveland became our home.

I don't think there is another city that has the kind of moral support and sense for artistic institutions that we have here — or the financial support for that matter, whether you're asking for five million or five dollars. When I see the huge crowds that come to see us; like the folks who came down to Public Square for the concert and fireworks on Fourth of July weekend, or the crowds crammed on the lawns at Blossom Music Center, that's not only interest, that's moral support.

And when you go around town, running errands to the drugstore or dry cleaners, and somebody asks you where you work, and you say the orchestra — they get very interested. First of all, they probably don't meet somebody from the orchestra every day. It's a different kind of job. But it's more than that. Everybody seems interested in the orchestra, and everybody is proud of the orchestra.

That means we in the orchestra feel an intense responsibility to the people of Cleveland. The people support us when we go on international tours. They support us at Severance Hall every night. I can't begin to tell you what that means to the people in the orchestra.

It makes for a wonderful work ethic. We are always going to do our best.

My life does revolve around University Circle with the orchestra and the Institute of Music down the street where I teach. But there's a lot more to this town than music. You also have the Cleveland Botanical Garden and the Cleveland Museum of Art. How many places in the United States have an art collection like that? And it's free! There are also a lot of great restaurants in this town.

To put it simply, my wife Gwen and I just love it here. We have two daughters; Alexandra is 20, but Nicole is just four. So we're also starting to rediscover the city, doing all the cultural and tourist kinds of things, seeing it through the eyes of our little one.

I mentioned how nice the spring was the first year I came here. But Aprils here can also be rainy. My favorite time of year is September and October — especially when the leaves turn. As happy as I am to go out and play in Vienna for a couple of weeks, I really miss that time of year when I'm on the road. There are some times of year you don't miss, like February. I'd rather do all our touring then, but unfortunately, that's not how the concert world works.

When I am here in September and October, I like to drive out to the country. I live in Shaker Heights, so we usually just drive out Shaker Boulevard to get some nice homegrown tomatoes, corn or apples from all the orchards out there, or just enjoy the beautiful scenery.

And when you go around town, running errands to the drugstore or dry cleaners, and somebody asks you where you work, and you say the orchestra — they get very interested. First of all, they probably don't meet somebody from the orchestra every day.

There are also a lot of golf courses around Cleveland. I love to golf, but I'm not that good. We actually have some pretty good players here in the orchestra. Let's just say, I don't hold them up too much.

Cleveland's also a very easy town to get around in. From Shaker, I can get [to Severance Hall] in 15 minutes. And if there's some sort of backup, I just jump over a block and I'm still on my way.

So yes, the orchestra is the main reason I came here. But since I've been here, I've also realized how much more Cleveland, my home, has to offer — the restaurants, the countryside in fall, the cultural amenities, Severance Hall, the Institute of Music and University Circle, which is where I spend much of my time. But most of all, I have come to know the people —those great people who support us and all the artistic and cultural institutions in this town. ✐

William Preucil, Concertmaster, The Cleveland Orchestra. Photographed at Severance Hall.

richard Gildenmeister

Cleveland has always been my "Big Apple." And I've had the best job of anybody in the city of Cleveland. That's a pretty big statement, but I can honestly say I've had an opportunity that very few people in the city of Cleveland have had — to meet so many great people. I've worked with over 9,000 writers during my career as a bookseller.

As my sister says, "Dick, you didn't make an awful lot of money, but you certainly have the riches from all the people you have met and all the people who respect you."

She's right. The book business has opened doors for me that never would have been opened. But none of it would have happened if it hadn't been for one Christmas when I was nine years old.

As a kid, I lived in a little farm town called Bellevue, Ohio, 75 miles west of Cleveland. During the holidays, my parents would always bring us here to see the lights. We'd go to the department stores: Halle's, Higbee's, May's and Sterling Linder.

One year, when I was nine years old, my father had brought us to town to see the Christmas lights and we were just starting home. He was heading down Euclid Avenue, and I started to whine. I said, "Some kid told me there's a place called Shaker Square where the lights are just beautiful." And my father, who didn't like to drive in Cleveland traffic anyway, said, "Well, we'll just have to find this Shaker Square place." I still remember him swinging that big car around right in the middle of Euclid Avenue.

It was the first time I saw Shaker Square. I fell in love with it instantly. Little did I know that one day Shaker Square would become my universe. It still is to this day. I've lived most of my life on Shaker Square since I've lived in Cleveland.

On Labor Day in 2005, it will be exactly 50 years to the day that my mother dropped me off in Cleveland at the YMCA — right on East 22nd and Prospect where it still is to this day. That's where all the boys from small towns took a room when they came to the big city. It was great. Downtown Cleveland was magic, alive and hopping.

I was hired at Higbee's and went through their junior executive training program. They moved me around to various places in the store, until I finally landed a job in the bookstore. That's where I met an incredible woman named Anne Udin.

She was born in Russia and was a real maverick for her time. She was the first bookseller to promote Dr. Seuss back in 1938, and all the librarians boycotted her because they thought Dr. Seuss was a "flit" book writer. They didn't take him seriously. At any rate, she took a liking to me and took me under her wing. She asked me if I wanted to learn the book business, which I did, because I liked the stimulation of it. It was something new every day.

So I lived at the Y and would walk every day during good weather down to Higbee's, which was down on Public Square — and it was a wonderful walk. In those days, Prospect was a very interesting street.

There were little restaurants, shops and pubs all the way down the street. And I got to know all of them.

Every night was Saturday night. I got involved with a crowd who liked to go out after work, and they just took me along.

I moved out near University Circle for a short time because a college friend of mine was doing an apprenticeship at the Cleveland Play House. My apartment on East 87th between Euclid and Chester had only one entrance. You had to go up the fire escape and through the bathroom to get in.

Thank God no one famous came there, just my friends from the Play House. But it was fun — you could walk to the Miami Restaurant and there was La Cave and Moe's Main Street where Johnny Ray had come.

But like I said, my career is more about who I've met. Helga Sandburg is one of my favorite writers. I met her here in 1956. I was her escort for one day and from that day on we became good and close friends. This was even before she met Dr. George Crile.

Jacqueline Susann was one of my staunchest supporters. I promoted her when I was at Higbee's after she wrote *Every Night Josephine*, which was about her poodle. No one knew who Jackie was back then, but I promoted her book and we became good friends. Every time I went to New York, she would invite me to the Plaza Hotel where I'd meet her and her husband, promoter Irving Mansfield, for cocktails and dinner.

Then she wrote *Valley of the Dolls*, and everyone knew who she was. Back then, she was neck and neck on *The New York Times* bestseller list with one of my favorite authors, Truman Capote, who had just come out with *In Cold Blood*.

> **I can honestly say I've had an opportunity that very few people in the city of Cleveland have had — to meet so many great people. I've worked with over 9,000 writers during my career as a bookseller.**

She and Irving weren't happy that Capote was ahead of them on the list, so they hired people to take their own poll, which of course showed that *Valley of the Dolls* was outselling *In Cold Blood*. So they marched into *The New York Times* and threatened to sue them, using their numbers. The next week their numbers rose.

Jackie and Irving were a force to be reckoned with. But I loved her and she called me on every birthday and at New Year's. She was a great friend and a bright light in my life.

I eventually met Truman Capote as well. A lady by the name of Adele Silver brought him in for a lecture series at Cuyahoga Community College. I brought my books to be signed and met him after his talk. I thought I'd died and gone to heaven.

But the biggest rush of my career was when I opened the Richard Gildenmeister Bookshop on the Square right in Shaker Square. It was important because back then, Shaker Square was in something of a fragile position — it had been declining. It needed a shot of new blood.

Richard Gildenmeister, Master Bookseller.
Photographed at the Reading Garden of the Cleveland Public Library.

If anything, I was able to do just that.

The store opened on December 6, 1976. It was a clear day, and the night before we worked right up to the deadline trying to get books up on the shelves and tables. We had all kinds of volunteers — a lot of famous people, doctors from the hospital, their wives. To be truthful, I probably had more volunteers than people who actually got paid.

The next day, everyone was there. We had a ribbon and a red carpet that went all the way out to the street. It was nine o'clock in the morning when TV5 news analyst Dorothy Fuldheim came to cut the ribbon. She had on a white ermine fur coat and black satin slacks with white dragons embroidered on the sides.

I had sent invitations out all over town, and all over the map, to people I had known — and most of them showed up. Ruth Ratner Miller promised to bring Mayor Perk. And by golly, he showed up and stood on a little box and even gave a speech. Barbara Walters sent congratulations saying, "The store was the best news to come out of Cleveland in a long time."

My folks came from Bellevue, along with my family, and the mayor of Shaker Heights, Walt Kelly, was there. We were swamped the entire day. At night we had Kleig Lights shining into the skies out in front until 11:30 — we really put on a show.

When I finally closed the doors and walked across the street, it was one o'clock in the morning. It had been clear all day, but as I walked across Shaker Square, a soft snow began to fall. That was the Shaker Square I fell in love with — that I had given my heart to. It's never left me.

Unfortunately, my store closed in 1981. But I still work as a master bookseller. I still live in the same apartment I have lived in for the past 37 years.

Even though my store isn't open today, I still believe I'm the luckiest person in town. How much more gratification does one need than when someone comes back to you and says, "Richard, I just loved the book you recommended." For me, my mission as a master bookseller has always been to bring the reader and the book together.

If I do that, it's a good day.

Then she wrote *Valley of the Dolls*, and everyone knew who she was. Back then, she was neck and neck on *The New York Times* bestseller list with one of my favorite authors, Truman Capote, who had just come out with *In Cold Blood*.

...so they hired people to take their own poll, which of course showed that *Valley of the Dolls* was outselling *In Cold Blood*. So they marched into *The New York Times* and threatened to sue them, using their numbers.

Want to hear something strange? An interesting little Cleveland-ism? I was born at Bayview Hospital — where Sam Shepard practiced medicine. And guess who delivered me? His brother Richard Shepard.

It didn't stop me from being happy growing up in North Olmsted. From my front yard on Ranchview, I could see Great Northern Mall being built. There was nothing along Lorain Road; you could see all the way across to the construction site. Now there's store after store, a Bob Evans and just about everything under the sun. It's grown so much.

Going to church at St. Richard's, my mom always sang — not in the choir or anything, just in the pew. She had a beautiful voice. My dad sang, too. I went to school at Coe Elementary at the corner of Columbia and Lorain and was in the choir by third grade. I still remember the soprano parts from "The Sound of Music." People don't believe me until I sing it for them.

When I was growing up, I never thought too much about being a journalist. To be truthful, I wasn't sure what I wanted to do. I went to high school at North Olmsted and was involved in everything — class president, president of student council and a cheerleader. I was on the swim team and ran track.

I ran the 440 and 880 relays, but I started out doing the hurdles. That was a nightmare. I didn't start track until I was in ninth grade, and I was so nervous the first time I ran the hurdles. We got down in the blocks and the girl next to me did a false start, so we had to start over. I was shaking like a leaf. Then, when the race started, I hit a hurdle with my lead leg and went down. And we had a cinder track back then. I was so worried, all I could think of doing was getting back up and finishing the race. My mother was at the end of the track by that time. She looked at me and said, "Come on, we're going to the hospital."

I looked down and my knees were just dripping with blood. I finished the race, but probably ripped my knees open more in the process.

You know where she took me? Bayview Hospital.

Like I said, I really didn't have a career in mind, so I took secretarial classes in high school. My mom told me to learn how to type, because you can always fall back on it. So I took cooperative office education. I got a job in the office at school helping out part-time. I also worked for a short time at Great Northern Mall at Foxmoor, which was right next to the Casual Corner.

Then I decided to go to Dyke College downtown for one semester. During that semester, I met Carl LaCava, a professor who taught some classes at Dyke. He was friends with a news anchor who worked at Channel 8 named Tana Carli. So he brought her to school to talk about her job one day, and I thought, you know, I could do that. It just sounded really interesting. Carl LaCava took five of us kids to lunch with her after her speech, and she was just so very

encouraging. She made me feel like I could do it.

That's when I decided to get into journalism, and that's when I switched schools. I wanted to go to Ohio State for journalism, but I couldn't get in until fall. So I took a few classes at Cleveland State that I knew would transfer and waited until fall.

Once in Columbus, I got an internship with the local ABC station. I interned for one quarter, then got a job there part-time as a desk assistant. Then I became a full-time news promotions producer while I was still in college.

I graduated from Ohio State and came back here, starting out as a reporter trainee at Channel 8 — a one-year position with no guarantees. They could fire me at any time if I wasn't working out. After that one year they signed me to a three-year contract and I ended up staying at Channel 8 for eight years. During that time I was promoted to morning anchor of the Newscenter 8 "This Morning" show, and eventually worked my way up to world and national anchor. Finally, I got the 6 p.m. and 11 p.m. spot. I left Channel 8 before it became Fox, and joined Channel 19 when it became CBS. And that's where I am today.

Being a television journalist is a privilege. As a Christian, I sincerely believe God has given me this job for a reason. The most rewarding part of my job is that I can bring attention to causes like Make-A-Wish, or Cornerstone of Hope, which is a new grief-counseling home that's being built in Independence.

I used to do a wish a week for Make-A-Wish. We featured a different wish kid each week. Their stories are inspiring, too. I mean, when you see a six-year-old battling cancer, what can you possibly have to complain about?

As I said before, I really feel like God has given me this job for a reason. It's a gift and it's up to me to use this gift. If I don't use it to help people, then why do I have it? I love that part of my job.

> I was so worried, all I could think of doing was getting back up and finishing the race. My mother was at the end of the track by that time. She looked at me and said, "Come on, we're going to the hospital."

But there are times when this job is a real challenge. The most challenging stories involve people you know. Those are the most difficult, because you have a special interest. The one that was the most difficult for me was the bombing of the U.S.S. Stark in the Persian Gulf in spring of 1987.

A friend of mine, Martin Supple, was on that ship. He was a lovely guy. This was a man who was involved in CYO at St. Richard's — a family man. We went on retreats and were in "Godspell" together when we were in high school.

So one morning I walk into work and I hear Mike Creagan, a reporter for Channel 8 who had this great voice, mention something

Denise Dufala, anchor of
Channel 19's "Action News."
Photographed at North Olmsted
High School.

about North Olmsted on the air.

"What's going on in North Olmsted?" I asked afterward.

"One of the sailors on the Stark was from North Olmsted," he said.

"Who?"

"Supple."

And I just froze.

"Danny or Martin?" I asked, because his brother Danny was also in the Navy.

"Martin."

Martin Supple was one of the last among the dead to be identified. He took a direct hit. People have short memories. They forget how Saddam Hussein bombed that ship in the Persian Gulf. So today I feel differently about us being at war in Iraq, because he killed my friend.

Naturally, because I knew the family, Channel 8 sent me out to the house. It was very difficult. His wife was also from St. Richard's. She had recently lost a baby — so it was just a devastating time for the whole family.

You get there, and you're their friend, and there are all these other reporters there. And you just want to say, "get out of here, leave them alone," but then you have to cover the story as well. In retrospect, I'm glad I was there, because I could tell people who Marty was.

But it was the hardest thing I ever had to do.

I was born at Bayview Hospital —
where Sam Shepard practiced medicine.
And guess who delivered me? His
brother Richard Shepard.

Being a television
journalist is a privilege.
As a Christian, I sincerely
believe God has given
me this job for a reason.
The most rewarding part
of my job is that I can
bring attention to causes
like Make-A-Wish, or
Cornerstone of Hope...

marlin Kaplan

When I came here in 1991, it was complete culture shock. I was living in Manhattan and was working at Sfuzzi, which had opened several restaurants across the country, including one in Tower City. I was essentially sent here to help get that operation up and running. But I was coming from a restaurant that had about $8 million a year in sales to the one here that did about $2.6 million in sales — so the restaurant here was about a third of the size of the one I was used to.

There were other things that were different as well. Each area of the United States has dishes that are indigenous to that area. In Cleveland, it's the seafood. It threw me a curve. I had swordfish and fresh tuna on the menu, and it just wasn't being embraced like it would be in New York. Then someone told me about walleye. I ordered 10 pounds the first night, and we sold out in about 10 minutes. I ordered 20 pounds the next night, and that sold out in 15 minutes. So I learned a lot about what walleye and even perch mean to this area.

Cleveland is a meat and potatoes town, but it really has grown up — especially from a culinary standpoint. Cleveland diners are starting to develop a very sophisticated palate — much more than they are given credit for — and they are starting to embrace more alternative forms of dining. I'm just happy that I was here to witness much of the transformation.

When I came here in 1991, there was really nothing downtown except Tower City. I would work at Sfuzzi and walk home to West 6th where I lived, and it was basically a ghost town. I lived in the Bradley Building, which was by Lakeside and West 6th. Back then, there was just the Burgess Grand Cafe, a dirty book store and then the Terminal Tower. But within a year or two, Cleveland was starting to come alive. Johnny's bought the Burgess Grand Cafe and turned it into Johnny's Downtown. Bars popped up at the end of West 6th. And the dirty book store moved. So in 1992 and 1993, night life was starting to creep into the Warehouse District.

Then the Indians moved to Jacobs Field and became a force. I was about to leave town right about that time, when a friend suggested I open my own restaurant here. I was literally watching the city grow up around me, so I decided to stay. I opened Marlin in what was once called the Guard House on East 6th Street. We tore off the front, put on a new facade, and created a little sidewalk cafe — which hadn't been seen too much in Cleveland before. In New York, just about every restaurant has French doors that open onto the street, but in Cleveland we were somewhat unique. It became a real focal point of the neighborhood. It became a real successful little restaurant, and even won some national acclaim.

Then the city really started to blossom. In 1995, the Indians became a real force and a lot of national attention was focused on Cleveland. Then the Rock and Roll Hall of Fame and Museum opened, and I knew it was time to branch out. I always wanted a barbecue place, so I opened a restaurant called Pig Heaven, which was right down the street from Marlin. Then a couple of years later, I opened my Italian restaurant Lira in 55 Public Square — so I had three restaurants.

The city was alive. The Gund was built, we had the NBA All Star game, and they were starting to build Cleveland Browns Stadium.

Over the next couple of years, we fell on some hard times. I had to close some of the restaurants down, but Cleveland has still been very good to me.

I had swordfish and fresh tuna on the menu, and it just wasn't being embraced like it would be in New York. Then someone told me about walleye. I ordered 10 pounds the first night, and we sold out in about 10 minutes.

I opened this restaurant after my landlord at Marlin suggested I move to One Walnut. This restaurant is essentially a grown up version of Marlin, more sophisticated and a little more varied. I've also changed the menu to be completely prix fixe — selling meals by the course, rather than by the item. At first our staff thought we would be committing suicide, but then they have seen how it's catching on.

Like I said, it's been fun watching Cleveland grow up and become more sophisticated. I feel like my restaurant here at One Walnut has grown up right along with the town.

So in 1992 and 1993, night life was starting to creep into the Warehouse District.

Marlin Kaplan, chef and restaurateur.
Photographed at his restaurant, One Walnut.

linn Sheldon

I 've been an entertainer for more than 42 years, and even though I've performed in many plays and in nightclubs, Barnaby is how most people know me. I took the name from a stagehand who had recently lost a dog by that name. I still get people who come up to me today and thank me, tell me that they remember me, or tell me what a big part I played in their childhood. It amazes me that so many people remember after all of these years.

To tell truth, I don't remember too many of the shows, because we never wrote anything down — it was all spontaneous. The stagehands would put some props on the table, maybe two or three, not too many, and I would go out and put on a show. Many times, I wouldn't know what the props were before I walked out on stage. If I had any talent, that was it: making up a story or a show using only a couple of small props.

One day, I came on stage and there was a large trunk. So I opened the trunk and inside there was an empty birdcage. Well right there, Longjohn, the world's only invisible parrot, was born. I never did ventriloquism; I just kind of faked my way through it, but it really didn't matter because the children's imagination took over.

The funny thing is, he became something of a foil for me, playing jokes on me and talking back. He quickly became a permanent part of the show. We did all kinds of skits with him. We even had a wire hooked up to a phone receiver so he it would look like he was answering the phone during the show.

Children have the most wonderful imaginations. They really took to Longjohn. Even some of the parents got into the act. I remember getting a call from one guy — I don't know whether he's serious or not — and he asks, "What's with all this invisible parrot stuff?"

And I say, "Well, you know, sometimes children like to have invisible friends."

So he says, "Yeah, but my kids got an invisible giraffe."

"That's nice," I say.

"Yeah, but now he's lost."

"Did you look on the lawn?" I joke.

"No, the lawn's full, he's not there."

"Why don't you look in the attic?" I suggest.

"Don't be silly," he says. "The attic isn't tall enough for a giraffe!"

One time, this was back in the mid-'60s when Ralph Locher was mayor, we had a parade downtown with Barnaby, Longjohn and 8,000 children — each with his or her own invisible pet.

It was a Saturday and we started at Public Square. I remember one boy came with an aluminum ring welded together, and it was around the neck of his invisible elephant. Then there was another kid tagging along behind him with a paper bag and those were the invisible peanuts for the elephant. We had judges and gave out prizes, and it was a hell of lot bigger than I ever thought it would be.

The winner was this boy who sat on a wagon with two reins and a bridle made of wood. Behind him was a stagecoach. It was being pulled by his imaginary horses. Of course, his brother was inside the coach peddling a bike. Children have the most amazing imaginations.

But some of the adults were downright scary. I used to get calls and letters from a man who said I had ruined his children's lives and that he was going to shoot me. This was back when Barnaby was really popular. I didn't really take it too seriously, because you get those kinds of things from time to time. So it was summer and we were going to have "Barnaby Day at Cedar Point." The day before, I get a call from this guy and he asks if I got his letters. I tell him I did, and he says, "Well I'll be at Cedar Point tomorrow and I'm going to kill you and I have a sawed-off shotgun to do it."

Well, now he's really got my attention. So I tell NBC and they tell the police. I fly out to Sandusky in a helicopter, and the State Police took me from there to the park. They have this big stage set up and there are cops all over in front of the stage. I get up on stage, and I take the microphone and I just started walking back and forth across the stage as quickly as I possibly can. I'm thinking, "If you're gonna shoot me, you're gonna do it on the dead run."

So we put on the show and the kids love it, and I come back on stage for applause. When I finally get off, I go back to the police car, get in and say to the two troopers, "I'd like to thank you guys for doing this extra work for me. I can't believe you went to all this trouble."

And one trooper says, "You're lucky. The guy was 12 feet away from you."

> **...Barnaby is how most people know me. I took the name from a stagehand who had recently lost a dog by that name. I still get people who come up to me today and thank me, tell me that they remember me, or tell me what a big part I played in their childhood.**

I guess he had on an overcoat and was cussing. A woman in the crowd told a policeman that there was a man saying bad words in front of the children. When they arrested him, they found out he had a sawed-off shotgun under his coat. It turns out the guy never had any children. He had just gotten out of the Lima State Mental Hospital.

Another sad story was the time I went to visit this boy in the Burn Unit of Metro Hospital. They told me he was dying and when I went into the room, I couldn't even tell if I was looking at something human, until he opened his eyes and said, "Hi Barnaby."

You know how he got there? His dad got drunk and put some paper on him and lit it. His father hadn't even come to see him while he was there.

So I ask the boy, "What would you like? What would you like to have and I'll get it for you if I can."

And he said he'd like to have a nice pair of shoe rollerskates. So I called my daughter who was living in New York at the time and she went down to FAO Schwartz and picked up the best pair of skates

Linn Sheldon, "Barnaby." Photographed at his home in Lakewood.

she could find.

Two days later I went back to the hospital, and the kid's father was there, still a little stoned.

"I understand you were going to give my kid what he wanted," he says. "Well, he's changed his mind. He doesn't want the rollerskates. He wants $15,000 to go to college and I'm to hold it until he comes of age."

I felt like hitting him, but didn't. I dedicated a show to that little boy with the bad burns. It was the only time I ever dedicated a show to someone. The only good part about the story is that the little boy recovered.

I guess you have to take the bad with the good, and there was plenty of good — especially from the kids. I remember one story especially well.

When he was young, my son Perry used to watch Barnaby, but he never really grasped that I was Barnaby. It was when we were doing the shows on tape, and I would go in and tape an entire week in one day. He was about seven years old. We were sitting there watching Barnaby one day, and I asked him if he liked Barnaby, and he says, "Yeah." And I say, "I'm Barnaby." And he looked at me and says, "Oh sure." He didn't believe me at all.

His mother had died recently from cancer and I had a housekeeper who took care of him while I was working. One day I had a special

appearance at Halle's department store and I saw him and the housekeeper waiting in line to see me — and he still didn't recognize me. As he got closer, I could tell he was getting excited. So he walks up, puts his hand on my arm and sits down. And I say, "Hi Perry." and he says, "Pop! What are you doing here? It's not supposed to be you — it's supposed to be Barnaby! What are you doing here?"

I took him aside and I told him that Barnaby was a job, and he asked if he could stand by me. I never cried in a show or at an appearance, but I almost did that day.

He stood by me for the rest of the day. And when the children came up, if they were there too long, he would say, "thank you," and keep them moving. Sometimes the kids would come up, put their arms around me and kiss me, and he'd say, "That's enough." Finally, after a while, it got to him. He pulled on my sleeve and leaned over and said, "Papa, they all love you, but there's only one me, right?"

I hugged him. That was perhaps the most tender moment of my life.

I've been very lucky in my career, to have met so many wonderful children, to have made a difference in their lives. I'm lucky to have my wife Laura, my son, two daughters and four grandchildren. Who would have thought that a guy from the backwoods of Norwalk, Ohio, who left home at an early age, would enjoy such a wonderful career?

I've been an entertainer for more than 42 years, and even though I've performed in many plays and in nightclubs, Barnaby is how most people know me. I took the name from a stagehand who had recently lost a dog by that name.

...my son Perry used to watch Barnaby, but he never really grasped that I was Barnaby... He was about seven years old. We were sitting there watching Barnaby one day, and I asked him if he liked Barnaby, and he says, "Yeah." And I say, "I'm Barnaby." And he looked at me and says, "Oh sure." He didn't believe me at all.

george Voinovich

ooking out my office window in Cleveland, I could talk for three hours and still not tell you about all the buildings. There is a story in every one of them. From my home on Cleveland's east side, I can walk to the end of my street and still see the skyline. But perhaps the best place to see the skyline is from the Inner Harbor.

I have a small boat, a 21-foot Classic that my wife has been encouraging me to sell for years, but I refuse to get rid of it. I take my children and grandchildren out on the boat and we can look up East Ninth Street at the skyline and see how the city has been transformed.

I love the lake. When I first got into politics, the lake was the northern border of the district I served in the Ohio House of Representatives. Back then everyone was writing it off. It was the poster child for a dying lake. I made up my mind back then that I was going to fight the second Battle of Lake Erie. I was going to do everything in my power to bring back the lake. Today, it's incredible what we have been able to accomplish. And when I say "we," I do mean "we."

I believe that government is but one thread in the fabric of a community. In order to solve problems, you have to galvanize all the resources. When I was lieutenant governor of Ohio and was asked to come back here and run for mayor, I did so for several reasons. Number one, I felt we needed new leadership, but number two, I felt there were great resources here that were untapped and that could be put to work to help our city. Number three, I got a commitment from the business community that they would indeed help me. When you include my days as mayor and governor, I have had more help from the private sector than any other public official in America.

Together, we transformed the skyline of the city. But I'm even more proud of what we were able to accomplish in Cleveland's neighborhoods. You can't have downtown development without neighborhood development. And it was very rewarding. To see people becoming excited about what is happening in their neighborhoods, to see them taking pride and providing them the resources to rebuild. When I was mayor, we only had the Riverbend Condominiums. Today, we're seeing more housing starts in Cleveland than we ever have in recent times.

I have a lot of fond memories and good feelings about my time as mayor, of the people who I met in the neighborhoods and the business community — the wonderful people who I had working for me in City Hall. People who didn't have to come, but they came because they believed in what we were doing. It was genuinely a very special time for our city, and I look back on it with great fondness. The excitement of turning our city around — it was a wonderful feeling we all had. We were working together to prepare our city for the next century. Maybe

it was the best time we ever had—especially when you look at the hurdles we had to overcome — being the first city to go into default after the Depression. Going through the terrible recession in '79, '80 and '81 was rough. In 1982, I had to go to Ronald Reagan and get him to give us an emergency jobs bill for 1983. But we picked ourselves up by our bootstraps with *esprit de corps* and a can-do attitude.

I remember one night in particular. It was July 13, 1981, and we were illuminating the Terminal Tower. What a celebration that was. There were so many people on Public Square. It was one hell of a celebration. It was a very big deal because we were trying to get people to believe that we had a future. Another day that sticks in my mind is December 14, 1982, when we broke ground on the BP Building. Or the time on "Monday Night Football," when they called us the Comeback Team from the Comeback City. And of course, all the work that went into the Inner Harbor and the Rock and Roll Hall of Fame and Museum.

When I became mayor, my goal was to make my administration the beginning of a new era for this city. So that when we celebrated our bicentennial, we would not be celebrating Cleveland's past, but rather celebrating Cleveland's future and the good days to come. We've

> **Or the time on "Monday Night Football," when they called us the Comeback Team from the Comeback City. And of course, all the work that went into the Inner Harbor and the Rock and Roll Hall of Fame and Museum.**

accomplished a lot, but there's still a lot that needs to be done. Still, I'm very proud. On my last day as mayor I joined the Cleveland Growth Association in lighting up another building at night — City Hall. I was with the Growth Association's president, Bill Bryant, and said, "Just remember, when I left, the lights were on!"

Looking back, I wouldn't change a thing. I have been very lucky. Have I made mistakes? Boy I sure have. We all do. But I have never looked back. I have always looked forward.

To this day, I still have not had a private party in Voinovich Park. It's a great honor having a park named after you, especially one right on the Inner Harbor. And I appreciate all of the accolades I have received through the years, but like I said, I certainly didn't do it alone. This year, we're going to have a big party down there, and I'll bring all the kids and my grandchildren, too. My oldest granddaughter Faith is seven, so there are still a lot of things she won't be able to understand. But I still want to have them all down there, to look up at our beautiful skyline and share with them all of the things that happened when we transformed this wonderful town. ☙

*George Voinovich, U.S. Senator,
former Mayor of Cleveland
and Governor of Ohio.
Photographed at The Capitol,
Washington, D.C.*

margaret Wong

most of my legal practice involves immigration law, which is very personal for me. I remember coming here from Hong Kong. It was the end of the Vietnam era, and I came to Seattle on a student visa with very little money but very big dreams. The experience had a very profound impact on my career and my life.

Being from the Far East, I was very supportive of the war in Vietnam. I knew that if the communists took over, thousands would be murdered. But when I got to Seattle, I was in shock. On the television, I saw thousands of young people smoking pot and protesting the war. Where I came from it was an honor to be able to serve your country, so I just didn't know what to think.

I came to the U.S. with my sister, and we were in Seattle for only 10 days before we moved to Iowa. I liked it there. There was no racism because we were probably the first Chinese people they had ever seen. I went to work as a waitress to earn money for college. Then, in 1973, the U.S. Supreme Court made a ruling that allowed foreign-born nationals to become notaries and lawyers, so I decided to go to law school in Buffalo. Back then, only about 20 to 30 percent of law students were women, and there were only three Asians in the whole school, so I was something of a trailblazer.

I didn't really think that doors were closed to me, but when I graduated I did have some trouble finding a job. I looked for jobs in New York, Washington, D.C., just about anywhere that would take me, but in those days the federal, state and city governments didn't hire Chinese women. I ended up teaching at the State University of New York at Fredonia. From there I went back to Buffalo, where I worked for the Mayor's Office as chief legal counsel for the HUD program. I came to Cleveland because I got a job at what was then Central National Bank. This is where my dreams really started to take hold.

I have some very fond memories of my first days here. I used to take the train from the Terminal Tower all the way to Van Aken Shopping Center, which is at the end of the line. I lived in Chagrin Falls, so I took the Number Five bus all the way there.

We Chinese did everything in a group back then. That's how I met my husband. There were always 10 or 20 of us who went out and did things on the weekends or whenever we could find the time. His folks owned a laundromat, and his father worked for 11 years trying to save for the passage to get his family here. So, like I said, immigration is a very personal thing for me.

Of course, I never stopped working once I got here. As a young lawyer at a small law firm, I used to take time to listen to other court cases and learn trial techniques by watching other more experienced attorneys. I would call judges, and ask to be assigned as a second chair, or to an interesting case, just so I could continue to learn. I also took on a lot of work — work that didn't pay much — but it gave me a lot of experience.

> The people who come here from other countries are often very innovative people who bring with them skills and the desire to open businesses and employ people — which is good for our entire city. They also bring their dreams with them — dreams they hope to realize here.

Now, of course, my practice is very well known. We handle immigration cases for numerous chief executives and their families as well as other individuals. Just recently, I won two People's Republic of China asylums, both of them stowaways. In Cleveland, that's virtually unheard of — and I feel very good about it because it's not just good for them, it's also very good for our community.

The people who come here from other countries are often very innovative people who bring with them skills and the desire to open businesses and employ people — which is good for our entire city. They also bring their dreams with them — dreams they hope to realize here. That's where I come in. I know where they're coming from. ✎

There was no racism because we were probably the first Chinese people they had ever seen.

THIS IS A GOV... NOT OF MEN

*Margaret W. Wong, immigration attorney
and civic leader.
Photographed at the
U.S. Court of Appeals, Cleveland.*

harrison Dillard

t he most memorable and most satisfying race of my life was a race I lost as a senior in high school. That was many years ago.

I was born down where the main post office now sits about 80 years ago, so I've seen a lot of changes in this town. I saw it grow to more than a million people, and slide back to a little under a half a million today.

Back in those days, Cleveland was a lot different. There were certain stores and restaurants where African Americans weren't welcome. And you wouldn't see African Americans working in banks or at certain department stores.

I remember there was one restaurant on East 55th, I can't even remember its name today, but it was a small neighborhood restaurant and we weren't welcome there. If you went in, you would get waited on eventually, but you would be sitting a while. We'd go in there once in a while just to get under their skin. You remember those things, but they don't seem as important as you get older. And, of course, things have changed quite a bit.

I went to Kennard Junior High School, which has long since closed. It was right across from Portland Recreation Center on East 46th and Scovill Avenue. That's where I first met my idol, Jesse Owens. He had a job there. I had seen him in news reels running in Berlin, but this was the first time I actually had the chance to speak to him. I didn't know it then, but in a few years I'd actually have the chance to run against him.

It was 1941 and I was a senior at East Tech High School. I had built a pretty good reputation as a track athlete and our coach, Ivan Greene, who was an excellent coach by the way, told me that I could run against Jesse Owens in an exhibition race at the Salem Night Relays, which were held down in Salem, Ohio. It wouldn't be a real race, it would only be an exhibition, but I agreed.

So we loaded up and headed down to Salem on a Saturday night. We took a bunch of cars, and I rode along in the coach's car. It was one of those in-between spring nights we have here in Ohio — a nice night, but a little on the cool side.

The race was a 120-yard low-hurdle race. Of course, at that distance it normally would have been a high-hurdle race, but this was

...so I've seen a lot of changes in this town. I saw it grow to more than a million people, and slide back to a little under a half a million today.

just an exhibition, and of course it was Jesse Owens.

I won a lot of races that year. I went on to win the state championship and the city championship in both the high and low hurdles. It's funny, but I didn't qualify for the hurdles for the Olympics in England. I qualified for the 100 meters, and won a gold medal.

But I remember that night as one of the most special races of my entire career. I was running against my idol, Jesse Owens. He beat me, of course, but it's a memory I still cherish to this very day.

But I remember that night as one of the most special races of my entire career. I was running against my idol, Jesse Owens. He beat me, of course, but it's a memory I still cherish to this very day.

Harrison Dillard, four-time Olympic gold medalist.
Photographed at George Finnie Stadium,
Baldwin-Wallace College.

dr. floyd Loop

before I came here in 1968 as a resident, I had big plans for my career in thoracic surgery. But my professor at George Washington University was impatient with me.

"That's it," he said. "You're going to the Cleveland Clinic. They'll train you there and you'll come back here to do heart surgery for George Washington."

So I got in my Volkswagen and drove from Washington, D.C., to Cleveland. My first impression of Cleveland wasn't very good. Back then, the town looked a little like bombed-out Warsaw in World War II. But when I walked into Cleveland Clinic, I knew it was a very different place. I never left.

I joined the staff in 1971 as a cardiac surgeon, and was head of the department in 1975. In 1989, I became CEO of Cleveland Clinic. I've had a very successful career here, but I attribute most of it to being in the right place at the right time. That, and as CEO surrounding myself with the right people who really did most of the work.

But my real profession is that of a surgeon. Those early years were best of all, because the Clinic was at the forefront of all sorts of surgery — especially coronary artery surgery. And the Cleveland Clinic performed coronary artery surgery better than anyplace in the world at that time.

Being a surgeon is a very satisfying profession. It's an almost perpetual process; one success leads to another, and technical advances and technological developments in the field give you a long-term high — you just can't wait to get to work each day. I performed a lot of technically demanding cases—a lot of re-operations. Those were really huge cases, the ones that were most satisfying.

Surgeons who dwell on the fact that they are saving lives are a little too full of themselves. It's not exactly like saving someone from jumping over a cliff. You're really just prolonging someone's life — allowing them to have a better quality of life.

Still, I did have a couple of cases that were emotionally satisfying. Mostly you remember the odd little episodes. One was a little fellow from Chicago in his 50s who was scared to death. He had terrible coronary artery disease, and because his disease was so severe, I could tell he wasn't going anywhere fast.

Remember, this was before lipid-lowering methods, so surgery was the only alternative. But he was scared. I actually had to talk him into the operation. I was glad I did.

He not only survived, but it totally changed his life. I ended up working on his wife, and actually re-operated on him 20 years later. Remember, though, I wasn't the only one doing this. It was being done here and across the country by hundreds of other surgeons. But can you imagine yourself being in a profession where you can have that kind of an effect on somebody? It's very satisfying.

There are times, too, that what you do in the operating room not only changes the person's life but those around him. When I first started my practice here, a man from Mexico came to me. He was roughly 65 years old, and was a famous ophthalmologist. He told me he was at the end of his rope. He couldn't function because he had so much chest pain and angina.

When I looked at his arteriograms, I realized it was a fairly simple operation. We used an internal mammary artery as an internal thoracic artery graft to his anterior descending. And it was a success. Here was a man who was ready to sell his practice and retire disabled. He recovered and built a new eye center down in Mexico and practiced for another 20 years.

The operation wasn't exactly a technical tour de force, but it was amazing how the procedure changed his life. There are literally thousands of stories like that that one encounters over a lifetime. When you make a difference in someone's life, it is very satisfying.

At the end of 1989, after taking someone's place on the board of governors, not even being elected for a full term, one thing led to another and I woke up one day and I was the CEO of Cleveland Clinic. I didn't want to give up surgery, but I slowed it way down. I was only doing between 150 and 180 cases a year. Eventually, I had to walk away from it altogether.

As an administrator, the first year was pretty tough because the Clinic was having some financial troubles, mainly due to operational systems which could be fixed. I really didn't have the staff, so we recruited. We probably placed or started new jobs for about 50 people in the first five years. After the first year, the place began to turn around. The Health System was developed. Hospitals were acquired. We built two hospitals in Florida. In my 15th year, about six months ago, I asked the board of trustees to consider a succession plan. Because I think you can overstay your time. We had the best year ever in 2003 and we're going to have an even better year this year. So it's a good time to leave.

There have been quite a few accomplishments around here, such as the opening of the Eye Institute with Dr. Hilel Lewis, opening up hospitals

Surgeons who dwell on the fact that they are saving lives are a little too full of themselves. It's not exactly like saving someone from jumping over a cliff. You're really just prolonging someone's life.

in Florida, and, of course, the Research Institute and Medical School. I've also met some of the best people I've ever met in my life here, like Al Lerner. His untimely death was a real tragedy.

In the end, though, I'd have to say that my biggest accomplishment here has been to assemble a group of people around me, doctors, surgeons, executives and managers who really did all of the work. That is very satisfying.

Like I said, it's been a very rewarding profession and career. The board has picked my successor in Dr. Toby Cosgrove, and he's an excellent choice. I'm sure he'll lead the Cleveland Clinic on to bigger and better things. For me, it's time to simply walk away.

Dr. Floyd Loop, retired CEO and Chairman
of the Board of Governors, The Cleveland Clinic.
Photographed at the Intercontinental Hotel and
Conference Center, MBNA Amphitheatre, Cleveland Clinic.

john Ferchill

had an old-world Italian father who used to say, "It's best to get rich in the dark." Of course, what he meant was that it's never good to promote yourself. That if you're going to be successful, it's best to do it quietly.

When I look back on it, though, his words were prophetic. I became successful in spite of myself. I once even sold myself out of a job, and then turned down a job with a guy who would go on to become a legend in real estate. Talk about working in the dark.

But I guess none of us really knew what was going on back then.

It was the middle of the '70s, and of course things were a lot different than they are right now. I was working for a company called Building Systems, Inc., as the project manager for Park Centre — which went on to become Reserve Square. As a mixed-use entertainment, retail and residential property, Park Centre was way ahead of its time — maybe even 20 years ahead of its time. But it wasn't working back then and Building Systems wanted me to reposition the property and put it up for sale, which was supposed to take six months. It ended up taking more than four and a half years because it was so screwed up — I can't even begin to tell you how bad it was. It was extremely hard to reposition, but I eventually found a buyer, and it was in the form of this guy from Chicago who had just started a real estate company.

We hit it off right away, and worked through the details of selling the building over several months. We even started to have some discussion about whether or not I would be willing to work with him, and to tell the truth there was some interest. But he was a maverick, and the whole culture of his company was different from what I was used to.

Still, I managed to get the building sold — but there was one big catch. The building had a HUD mortgage on it. That meant we had to go into federal court to get the sale approved. So we meet with the attorneys here in town the day before court, and this guy from Chicago tells us he doesn't own a suit. I mean the whole time we were working together he's wearing jeans and a sweater. I just assumed he had a suit — but he didn't. Remember, it was the '70s, and these guys looked liked they'd be more at home on a motorcycle than in a board room.

That night we go over to Harry Weinraub's to buy him a suit, and he just picks up one of the first things he sees. It's this velvet suit with wide lapels, and when he puts it on, he looks like Little Lord Fauntleroy. He can see how I'm reacting and says, "All I need is a suit, right?" And I say, "You're right." I mean the guy just didn't care.

The next day we got approved and the sale went through — all with him there in his Little Lord Fauntleroy suit. He even offered me a job, but like I said, the culture wasn't right. This guy was a maverick and I grew up in a town of 10,000 — New Philadelphia — with two very Italian parents. Of course, the guy's name was Sam Zell, and he went on to become a legend in real estate.

Of course, what he meant was that it's never good to promote yourself. That if you're going to be successful, it's best to do it quietly.

After I made the sale, I went home and my wife and I decided to put all of our savings into starting a new company. We had $25,000 and we got a line of credit from a friend for another $25,000. The idea was that we would give it a year to see how it would work. Imagine that, a year to see if a company would work. It takes at least seven. And I had three little girls, all under the age of six. Talk about working in the dark.

It all worked out in the end, though. During my career, I've been able to develop more than $1 billion of real estate. And Sam, he of course owns a huge real estate company in Chicago — a living legend. But when I see him in magazines or on television, he still isn't wearing a suit.

Remember, it was the '70s, and these guys looked liked they'd be more at home on a motorcycle than in a board room.

John Ferchill, developer.
Photographed at the Northpoint Building,
downtown Cleveland.

kid Leo

Cleveland Municipal Stadium. It's gone now. Not many, if any, Clevelanders shed a tear when the wrecking ball hit its giant and foreboding edifice. But I took pause when I read of its impending demolition in *USA Today*. While I was residing in New York at the time, my heart and mind returned to Cleveland and memories of that grand old structure.

There were many historical moments, public and personal, that took place within those hallowed bowels that were part and parcel of what shaped my life. I also know that many of these same events were very important to the populace of Cleveland. The people just had a hard time getting over a reputation that the Stadium itself couldn't escape.

For the most part, Clevelanders remember infinitesimal crowds for bad baseball teams, heartbreak for those aficionados of the gridiron and a whipping wind off of Lake Erie that could make Dorothy's Kansas twister in "The Wizard Of Oz" feel like a gentle breeze. I, on the other hand, looked at it in as a "horse of a different color."

My childhood idols played the games that took place at Cleveland Municipal Stadium (Rocky Colavito was #1 on the hit parade) but my initial ingrained memory regarding the Stadium actually started at my home on a Sunday morning in November of 1963. I was going to the Browns game with my father and uncles. They were in the kitchen and I was in the living room watching TV. All of a sudden a shocking and yet intriguing image hit the screen. The man who was accused of assassinating John F. Kennedy was, himself, ambushed. I cried out to my dad and relatives, "Lee Harvey Oswald just got shot!" Of course, they weren't about to accept the excited word of a 13 year old, so they sloughed it off and said, "Yeah, right...get ready we're leaving soon." I was about to protest when all of a sudden the network announced it was going to show the Oswald shooting again. I yelled for all to come in and we witnessed the first use of instant replay we'd ever seen in our lives. We then left for the game shaken from everything that had happened that weekend. It was a different time and the general feeling (or spin) was "The President would've wanted the games to go on." The NFL said so. We believed so. The Cleveland Browns were playing the Dallas Cowboys that given Sunday. When the Cowboys took the field the boos raining down on them were the loudest I'd ever heard. They were taking the brunt for the fact that JFK went down in Dallas. They never were in the game and it was an all too easy win for the Browns. Even at my age I knew it was a hollow victory.

The next vivid recollection is from a little over a year later. It was another Browns game. But this wasn't just ANY game. No, this was an NFL Championship Game. However, the Browns were a double-digit underdog and no so-called expert was taking the points. We were dogged (and this is way before the "Dawg Pound") in our belief. And...it was truly unbelievable. Gary Collins caught three TD passes and the Cleveland Browns shut out the supposedly invincible Baltimore

Colts. As special as that day was, it became something altogether more important to me the next spring. On May 26 of 1965 my father died. That championship game was the last event we saw together at the Stadium. Dad...we went out winners.

We'll skip a bit forward to Memorial Day, 1977. I walk into the Stadium with my wife-to-be (Jackie) to see the Indians play the Angels. We are one batter late. There's a California Angel on first base. I hate missing a pitch. I'm anal and I like the now almost extinct art of keeping score. Yet, as I look up at the scoreboard, I see there are no hits on the tally. At that point in time, and you can check with my wife, I said, "Well at least Eck's still got a no-hitter." Indians' pitcher Dennis Eckersley had walked the first batter. By the time the game was over, the Angels did no further damage, the Indians got a cheap run off Frank Tanana and I played witness to a no-hitter along with about 12,000 others, which was ABOVE the norm for Indians attendance those days. It was a holiday after all. Because of the lack of attendees we slipped into seats behind home plate for the last four innings. It was something to see. I lay testimony to the fact that a no-hitter is the most exciting event in sports,,, where nothing happens. It happened at Cleveland Municipal Stadium.

There's a bit more. In 1980 I, in a moment of ultra-commercial lucidity, created on the airwaves of WMMS a catch-phrase that went by the name of "Siper Bowl." The Browns' quarterback was Brian Sipe. The goal was the Super Bowl. The combination of those two elements seemed...well...elementary. The city grabbed onto that phrase and rallied around it. I got a lot a kudos for thinking of it except from the sportswriters of the time who couldn't believe a Rock 'n' Roll DJ would relate to their supposedly captive audience better than they could.

In 1980 I, in a moment of ultra-commercial lucidity, created on the airwaves of WMMS a catch-phrase that went by the name of "Siper Bowl". The Browns' quarterback was Brian Sipe. The goal was the Super Bowl.

Every game that year saw banners boasting "Siper Bowl Bound" plastered all over the Stadium. It got the city into a frenzy until on the coldest day you could imagine it all ended...totally and dramatically. In the divisional playoff game against the Raiders, Cleveland wound up one play short...at the goal line...with time running out...when a field goal would've secured victory...but a pass was attempted...and intercepted. A team and a city left just inches from moving closer to the "Siper (Super) Bowl" that they could've, should've won.

Before you think it's all about sports, let me tell you we set the city (and I might add, the rest of the Rock 'n' Roll industry) on its collective butt by putting on a series of concerts that became a model for promoters across the country. WMMS's partner was one of the most respected concert management organizations in the country, Cleveland's own Belkin Productions. The concept was called "The World Series Of Rock." I had the duty of acting as the MC for the initial

Kid Leo, radio personality.
Photographed at Patsies Restaurant, Manhattan.

kid Leo

event. There can't be anything comparable to walking out onto a stage in front of 80,000 people, ready to pee in your pants, and have them cheer and applaud as you introduce yourself. One of the sweetest sounds I'd ever heard. It almost left me speechless...but not quite.

The names of the Rolling Stones, Bob Seger, Pink Floyd and Bruce Springsteen are only a few who made that Cleveland Municipal Stadium marquee shine. I spent a lot of time "on the field" as a participant and contributor to concerts that made the city of Cleveland secure its reputation as the "Rock 'n' Roll Capital of the World."

There are many more memories (I will not delve into that infamous drive by John Elway that really put a stake through the heart of Cleveland) that could be chronicled...but there is a final great moment in Cleveland Municipal Stadium's life that is tied together with mine.

It happened on Labor Day of 1995. During my last years at WMMS, I was very involved with the campaign to have the Rock and Roll Hall of Fame and Museum located in Cleveland. It was a long and hard-fought fight. Cleveland won the battle but, oh what a war was yet to be waged. The city was granted the rights to the Rock Hall in 1986. What followed that decision wasn't pretty, but after nine years of kicking, biting, scratching and whatever else the situation demanded, Cleveland proudly opened that Rock and Roll Hall of Fame and Museum with a concert to

end all concerts. You name 'em...they were there. A veritable "Who's Who of Rock 'n' Roll" entertained a sold-out crowd. The audience gave as good as they got. On a night when I would've been honored just to be there, I was invited back to my hometown to open up the evening's festivities as host of the "Concert for the Rock and Roll Hall of Fame." I walked up on that stage, six and a half years after leaving for a job in New York, swelling with pride, joy and just a plain old happiness that made me grin from ear to ear (an ugly sight). The crowd responded with an ovation that will be with me beyond the grave.

A year later, the fortunes of Cleveland Municipal Stadium had taken a turn for the very worst. The Cleveland Browns snuck out of town...literally. Art Modell sold out the city. The Indians, who never really could make the Stadium work, had the good fortune to be blessed with a godsend and a Godfather...Jacobs Field and Dick Jacobs. Great for the Tribe and the city. Not exactly what the "old lady" needed. The NFL rebuked Modell and gave Cleveland a new (yet historical) Browns team that would generate the funds to build a modern football stadium. Another blow. The last resort of flea markets and religious crusades thankfully weren't a factor. It was time to go.

It's gone. But, at least in these quarters it still stands...and stands tall.

By the time the game was over, the Angels did no further damage, the Indians got a cheap run off Frank Tanana and I played witness to a no-hitter along with about 12,000 others...

I walked up on that stage, six and a half years after leaving for a job in New York, swelling with pride, joy and just a plain old happiness that made me grin from ear to ear (an ugly sight). The crowd responded with an ovation that will be with me beyond the grave.

mary rose Oakar

Cleveland is fortunate because it's a cultural mosaic. Our neighborhood was very diverse, kids from all kinds of backgrounds. That was the greatest part of growing up in Ohio City.

When I campaigned for City Council in 1973, I would go to a little street behind St. Malachi's Church in the Flats called Mulberry Street. One family was Irish, one was Hungarian, and one was African-American, all there for generations living next door to one another. In fact George Michael Moore, an African-American journalist who grew up in Ohio City and went to St. Patrick's and St. Ignatius, spoke fluent Hungarian because he grew up next door to people who were originally from Hungary.

So it was a very diverse neighborhood. It still is in many ways. And it's one of most historic neighborhoods in all of Cleveland. Ohio City used to be a separate town until it merged with Cleveland. It was Ohio City from 1836 until 1854, when a guy named William Castle, who was mayor of Ohio City, proposed a merger with Cleveland but cut a shrewd deal. As part of the merger, he became mayor of Cleveland. So Castle was the first mayor after the merger of the two cities. He lived in a huge mansion on Franklin Boulevard — the county owns it now. He's buried in the cemetery at 30th and Monroe, just south of Lorain.

If you look down Franklin, that's where the wealthy once lived, people like the Hannas and Frances Payne Bolton. President Garfield was once a preacher at the Franklin Circle Church. The Underground Railroad stopped at St. John Episcopal Church on Church Avenue — which is the oldest church in Cleveland.

So Ohio City has a terrific history.

Even though I've been in the U.S. Congress and worked in Washington, D.C., I've lived in Ohio City all of my life. I still do.

I remember going to the West Side Market with my father when I was three. I still go there every weekend, or every other weekend when I'm home. It's a consumer's dream and the best market I've ever seen. And I have been all over the world, or at least a good part of it.

Growing up in Ohio City, we didn't have a lot of parks or open spaces, and the yards are small. So our family would get together and go to Edgewater Park or over to the old Municipal Stadium to watch baseball.

My fondest memories are of the 1948 baseball team. I can still tell you who was on that team to this day. I was the youngest of five kids. My dad would pile us in his old Jeep and we'd sit on a blanket behind the fence in the outfield. We watched the World Series there, which was real big.

I loved sports because I had three older brothers. They were the All-Oakar basketball team. My sister liked sports, too, so we followed them around quite a bit.

We lived right across the street from St. Ignatius High School. Two of my three brothers went there. The Jesuits used to threaten to throw my brothers through the bay window if they didn't behave. They were always doing crazy things. So we grew up right across the street from the Jesuits and we owe a lot to them. I went to St. Patrick's on Bridge Avenue and then to Lourdes Academy, which is no longer there.

As you get older, you naturally become involved in other things. You're active, so you just come home and sleep and you don't pay much attention to what's going on around you. I was active in plays, directing plays and teaching at Tri-C and Lourdes Academy as a lay teacher, when my friend Tom Campbell (not Dr. Tom Campbell) came home to visit from California in the early '70s.

He lived just around the corner from me and his sisters are my best friends. He told me he counted more than 52 bars in our neighborhood. It was honky-tonk heaven, and going downhill. So we got a bunch of people together to see what we could do to save the old neighborhood.

We decided to do something about the person representing us on City Council, and everyone decided that I should be the one to run because I had always lived there. So that's how I got involved in politics, because my neighborhood was declining. It was a rough-and-tumble race, but I won.

> **We decided to do something about the person representing us on City Council, and everyone decided that I should be the one to run because I had always lived there. So that's how I got involved in politics, because my neighborhood was declining.**

Today, my best friends are the people I grew up with in Ohio City. The people I went to grade school and high school with are my best friends to this day. My brother formed a club of the people who grew up in the neighborhood and the whole gang still gets together once a year. Everyone's getting older, they bring their children and grandchildren — but it's that kind of loyalty to our old neighborhood that really makes Ohio City special.

I would have never won any of my elections without the support of my neighborhood pals. The neighborhood where I grew up has had an enormous influence on me and gave me a tremendous love for the City of Cleveland.

It's still my favorite place to live.

Mary Rose Oakar, former congresswoman.
Photographed at the Women in War Monument at Arlington National Cemetery.

phil Donahue

n the darkened Riverside Theatre on Lorain Avenue at Kamms Corners, some time in the late '40s, a cop quietly approached me from behind and with a loud rap of his flashlight on the back of my seat said, "Do your necking at home, pal!"

You don't forget these things.

Such was my big, fat Norman Rockwell life growing up on the West Side after the war. No drugs, no gangs, just dutiful Cleveland police ready to engage in *in loco parentis* anytime, anywhere — even if the underage citizen was breathlessly involved in a mutually consensual kiss.

I came of age in Cleveland at the same time Major League Baseball came of age. Larry Doby was as brave as Jackie Robinson (without the lifetime of adulation). We also had Lou Boudreau, a 24-year-old player-manager with a matinee-idol face who pulled pitchers in and out of the line-up from his own shortstop position. And Spanish-speaking players were beginning to appear in our line-up.

The Bill Veeck Indians were different. We had Feller, Gordon, Lemon and Keltner (who stopped DiMaggio's 56-game hitting streak). Luke Easter and Pat Seery also wore the smiling Indian along with Al Rosen, a Jewish third baseman.

We also boasted about Emil Bossard, the best groundskeeper in the big leagues.

Other memories that forever linger: Bobby Avila sliding into home plate and jarring the catcher's grasp. "I keeck the ball," he said, and all of Cleveland's white working-class neighborhoods rejoiced at the winning run.

Jim Hegan, the Indian's catcher, was very big in my parish. We were awed by the way he discarded his mask and made his way, without looking up, to the precise spot where the foul ball would come down, making the catch effortlessly. Our admiration was all the more personal because Jim Hegan was, in the jargon of my childhood, "a good Catholic."

It was the dark ages, a time when baseball players left their gloves on the field and World Series games were played only in daylight. Sister Bertrand at Our Lady of Angels School allowed us to listen to the World Series games on the radio.

It was 1948 and there we were, concentrating on every pitch as Jimmy Dudley and Jack Graney brought the big game right through the classroom door, past the crucifix on the wall and into the hearts and minds of the OLA eighth graders who lived and died with The Tribe.

Life was good for a Cleveland sandlot kid: stickball on Southland Avenue, fishing, trapping and scaling the shale walls of "The Valley" (otherwise known as Cleveland Metropolitan Park). These were the daily activities during my coming of age, an age before heavy metal—a soft, civil time of Montivani music at the St. Christopher Saturday Night Canteen in Rocky River, where all the girls wore angora sweaters.

Like being interrupted in the dark — amid-kiss — you don't forget these things. This was my Cleveland, the Best Location in the Nation — believed it then, believe it now.

I remember seeing my first television picture, the animated lighthouse logo of the Scripps Howard Company, owner of the local ABC station. As the beacon swept by the screen and returned again, the announcer, Cort Stanton, boomed, "WEWS, Channel Five, first in Cleveland."

And how lucky can a guy get. St. Edward, one of the nation's finest Catholic high schools for young men, opened just in time for me. I am a member of the first graduating class, 1953. We presided over the first of everything — football, band, school paper and commencement ceremony. For four years we strutted about like the "seniors" we always were, never a bully above us. Today, St. Edward High School, under the leadership of Brother Peter Graham, enjoys one of the finest reputations in the nation, in academics and athletics.

Like being interrupted in the dark — amid-kiss — you don't forget these things. This was my Cleveland, the Best Location in the Nation - believed it then, believe it now.

...a cop quietly approached me from behin back of my seat said, "Do your necking a

Phil Donahue, television personality.
Photographed in Central Park, New York.

nd with a loud rap of his flashlight on the
ome, pal!"

harvey Pekar

a lot of people have been talking about the success of *American Splendor*, but I can tell you success doesn't come easy. Nothing ever pours in — especially in comics. It's very difficult because the comics business is in really bad shape these days.

I got interested in comics when I was a kid, you know, the usual stuff like Captain Marvel and Plastic Man. I collected them, but when I got to sixth grade I got sick of them. They were formulaic, predictable — kid's stuff — and I was bored with them.

I wouldn't get interested in them again until I met Robert Crumb. Crumb was about four years younger than me. He was living in Philadelphia, got out of high school and couldn't find work. Crumb was corresponding with a friend who happened to live right around the corner from me. This guy, Marty Pahls, writes to Crumb and offers to make him his roommate. So Crumb came to Cleveland in 1962. He came here just to get out of Philadelphia. He got a job at American Greetings as a color separator. Crumb lived up on East 109th and Carnegie and I lived at 107th. This was back in the '60s.

It was the early days of the counterculture — a real exciting time. And a lot of exciting things were happening all around me. There were anti-war demonstrations, a lot of bohemians, and action on the street. There were definitely a lot of people running around doing all kinds of wild stuff, and Crumb and I were a part of it. At first, the mutual interest was mainly jazz. Crumb was a record collector and so was I, so we used to swap records. Crumb only liked the old stuff, from 1933 or before, but I liked be-bop and everything. That's how we got to know one another.

One day, Crumb showed me some of his artwork, and I was really impressed because it was excellent. I also noticed that it had an appeal to adults. It wasn't for kids, they wouldn't get it. That's when I started looking at comics differently. Maybe there was nothing wrong with comics at all. Maybe they were just being used the wrong way. No one was taking advantage of the fact that you could do anything with comics. All they were doing was this super hero stuff.

Because of Crumb's work and other early underground cartoonists like Harvey Kurtzman at *Mad*, I saw the potential to write adult comic-book stories. I theorized about it all the time before finally getting into it. It took me years before I wrote my first story. I wrote it out storyboard-style with balloons with dialogue and stick figures, because I can't draw worth a damn.

I drew a lot of my influence from people I saw around town. I would look for things that aggravated me — the small things in life, like getting stuck in a check-out line. I would just keep an eye out for things like that and write about them.

It was 1972, and Crumb had been living in California, but he came back here quite a bit. On one of those visits, I gave Crumb some of my work and asked what he thought of it. He said he liked the stories and would I mind if he took a few of them home with him so he could draw them. I was tickled pink, because Crumb was already a legend. He gave me instant credibility. I was off to a really good start and had all these plans to do longer, more ambitious stories. But then the Vietnam War came to a close. People quit supporting the counterculture after they found out they didn't have to serve in Vietnam. Everything dried up — and there I was. I had all these great ideas, but there was no place to publish them.

I really didn't know what to do. At the time, I was still a heavy record collector. I would spend thousands of dollars on records each year. So I decided to quit buying jazz records and put out my own comic book — if I lost money, I lost money. So that's how I put out my first *American Splendor* in 1976.

It was a real learning experience. I didn't know anything about printing. One of the artists I was working with was married to a woman who knew someone in the printing business. So I met him and he set me up with different people to get the comic book printed. The insides ended up being printed one place and the cover printed in another and then the whole thing was stapled together in some other place. After they were printed, I took them home and then had to call on these wholesalers to see if I could get any of my money back by selling them books.

> **So I decided to quit buying jazz records and put out my own comic book — if I lost money, I lost money. So that's how I put out my first *American Splendor* in 1976.**

But it didn't work so well. I didn't make any money for years. But I wasn't making any money collecting records either, so I stuck with it. Crumb did a cover for me in 1980, and not too long after that someone contacted me about doing a movie version. I would get sporadic requests for it, and a couple of times it was actually optioned, but it never really took off until HBO got interested in it almost 20 years later.

So that's how *American Splendor* was born. I published *American Splendor* just about every year until the early 1990s, when Dark Horse took over.

Now it's a movie and everybody's talking about it — but I can tell you it didn't come easy. It took a lot of money and a lot of time — but it's taken me a whole lot further than just collecting records.

Harvey Pekar, comic book writer.
Photographed at Tommy's in Cleveland Heights.

dick Feagler

've seen my share of funny things in this town. Most of my war stories have to do with reporting more than column writing.

Before I began my column, I was a reporter for the *Cleveland Press.* It was the mid-'60s. Back then, we all liked murders — especially good-address murders. The idea was, you didn't just report the murder, you caught the villain.

I had the opportunity to do it once. The woman actually told me she did it while I interviewed her on the front stoop — just not in so many words. But the experience wasn't as rewarding as I had hoped. Just strange and chilling.

It's 2:30 in the afternoon on a Tuesday. I'm on the rewrite and general assignment desk. The city editor, Louie Clifford, comes over to me and says, "Here's the deal. A woman called the cops in Shaker Heights at 9 o'clock this morning and said her 7-year-old son is missing. They just found him dead in a cul de sac off Gates Mills Boulevard. Go out and see the woman to see what you can dig up."

So I get the address, which is definitely a good address, and go out and knock on the door. A woman named Nancy Young comes to the door. I tell her I'm from the *Cleveland Press.* She says, "You came about my son. Have they found him?"

At that point I realized she didn't know her son was dead. Somehow we got it before she did. So I say, "Well ma'am, I just came out to get some particulars. But if you'd like me to, I'll check back just to make sure they haven't found him."

This was in the days before cell phones, car phones or anything else. So I go to the next-door neighbor's house and ask if I can use her phone. The woman says yes, but she's all distraught because she knows this kid is missing. Clifford gets on the phone, and I say, "Louie, the woman doesn't know and I didn't tell her. What do you want me to do? I don't want to break it to her."

While I'm on the phone, the cops come next door and I know they're telling her about her son. Louie asks me where I'm calling from and I tell him the next-door neighbor's house, a woman named Colby. He tells me to call him back. But the cops are there a long time, so I head back to the office.

The next morning, which is a Wednesday, I come in and Clifford says, "Why don't you go back and talk to the Colby woman again — you know, background stuff. What kind of kid was he? That sort of thing."

I go back out, but this time she doesn't let me in the house. So I interview her on the front porch and she talks to me. At this point, the story is almost like one of those bad jokes where somebody tells you something three times, and it always happens the same way three times except for the last.

Clifford sends me out there on Thursday, then again on Friday. By this time we're starting to talk about the most mundane subjects. Like the pachysandra in her yard and what she has planted in her garden. I'm on a total fishing expedition.

The next day is Saturday, and Clifford is off so I figure I won't have to go back out there. When I get in, there's a note on my typewriter: "Go out and see Mrs. Colby." So I did. Monday, he sends me out there again.

And once again, we're talking about the most innocuous topics. Until out of the blue she says, "Can I ask you a question?"

I say sure.

"The police have been around talking to us, do you think I should tell them about the bullet hole in my kitchen?"

"I don't know," I say. "How did you get a bullet hole in your kitchen?"

"Well, we have rats in the house, and we couldn't catch them, so I called the Shaker Heights police," she says. "They came over and a policeman saw a rat, so he pulled his gun and shot the rat, but he missed and now there's a bullet hole in the kitchen. The policeman made me promise not to say anything because he shouldn't have done it. Do you think I ought to tell them?"

And I say, "I wouldn't tell anybody about that, Mrs. Colby."

I get in my car, which is parked at her curb. I'm thinking about where I can find the nearest phone booth. Fortunately, I had grown up nearby. I knew there was a phone at the Van Aken Rapid Station at Van Aken and Lee. I call Clifford and tell him the woman just slipped up.

The police arrest her for questioning, which they hadn't previously done. They sweat her out, then let her go. They pull her in the next day, and on the second round of questioning she confesses. On the third day of questioning she tells the whole story, and here it is:

The Colby woman was kind of dotty. She was married to a wet schmuck of a husband who went up to the attic every night and played with a ham radio. She had one son, Dane Colby, who was the same age as the boy who was murdered. He wasn't retarded, but I guess he wasn't all that bright either.

Nancy Young was married to a good-looking yachtsman type. She was good-looking, too. Her son, John Kramer Young, was a good-looking kid, fast, real sharp. The Colby woman had a crush, an unrequited crush, on Nancy's husband.

Before I began my column, I was a reporter for the *Cleveland Press.* It was the mid-'60s. Back then, we all liked murders — especially good-address murders.

The Colby woman allowed John Kramer Young to play with her son every day. When he came in, she would set an alarm clock and when it rang he had to leave. The Colby house was one of those houses that had about two steps up to the kitchen from the side door. When John Kramer Young came over, he had to take his shoes off before he came in the house. He was so well behaved, he always did it.

John Kramer Young came over to her house that Tuesday to play with her son. When the alarm rang, John Kramer Young sat down on the kitchen steps to put on his boots like he always did. But Mrs. Colby walked into the living room, pulled a pistol from a coffee urn and shot him in the back of the head. She rolled him in a rug. Drove him to a

Dick Feagler, columnist and author.
Photographed at his home in Bay Village.

cul de sac on Gates Mills Boulevard. And dumped him out.

She came back and wrapped the pistol in ground meat and covered it with paper. She marked the package "meat loaf" and put it in the freezer — which is where the cops found it when she finally confessed.

When it was over, I went back to Clifford.

"How the hell did you know this?" I ask. "Why did you keep sending me back there day after day?"

It turns out Clifford had a friend in the Sheriff's Department. When they went over to interview her, she was crying — even before she knew why they were there.

Clifford made me cover the trial, too. With all those visits, I'd built a rapport with her. Every time she came into court, she'd smile and wave at me — with this sick sweet smile that put a pit in my stomach, raised the hair on the back of my neck, and sent chills up my spine.

Back then, Jerry Gold was a big noise in town — a public defender.

He got her off on insanity. The last I heard of her, she was a matron at some hospital down by Marietta.

I started at the *Press* in 1963, and was a reporter there for eight years before I began my column in 1971. Throughout it all, I've been blessed to have witnessed so much history.

I went to live with the hippies in Haight-Ashbury in May of 1967 and was in Vietnam in December the same year. When I was there, I realized that nothing they'd ever taught me applied to the situation there.

I was at Good Samaritan Hospital on deathwatch for Bobby Kennedy in June of 1968. And ran from the cops in Chicago during the Democratic Convention of 1968.

Like I said, I've seen my share of funny things. But that murder always sticks with me.

It still gives me the creeps.

"The police have been around talking to us, do you think I should tell them about the bullet hole in my kitchen?" "I don't know," I say. "How did you get a bullet hole in your kitchen?"

She came back and wrapped the pistol in ground meat and covered it with paper. She marked the package "meat loaf" and put it in the freezer — which is where the cops found it when she finally confessed.

michael Stanley

euclid Avenue. I try to tell my daughters about the bustling majesty that was the Euclid Avenue of my youth. I try, but I can tell it doesn't register.

In an earlier era, it had been known as Millionaire's Row, where names like Rockefeller, Hanna and Mather ran together and set the national standard for wealth and opulence.

Today as you walk the avenue from Public Square to Playhouse Square, you move through a corridor of vacant storefronts and once-proud buildings that hold the memories of a different time — a time when all of northeastern Ohio swirled around this concrete ribbon and looked for reasons to join the party. Today it's not quite yet a ghost town, but the reservations appear to have been made.

From the sheltered enclave of Rocky River, my friends and I would take the 55N (or hitch a ride on a slow-moving freight train if we were sure no parents were watching) down Lake Road to Clifton Boulevard, past Edgewater Park and into downtown. It was a journey that only took about 30 minutes but our destination might as well have been another land. If Lennon and McCartney had already written "Magical Mystery Tour" it would have been our theme song.

The bus would drop us off at Public Square and, beneath the shadow of the Terminal Tower (there couldn't possibly be a bigger building in the world, could there?) we would slide into a moving sea of humanity.

Under Higbee's elaborate window displays sat ragged men who sold pencils out of rusted cups, alongside a sunglasses-wearing hipster channeling Miles, Coltrane or Getz. And even though my "bankroll" was minuscule, the sounds from that tarnished horn started me on a lifelong habit of always throwing something in the case of those who play for free.

The aroma from the nut shop on Euclid near Ontario would pull you eastward past the record store, The May Company and toward what seemed like an endless string of movie marquees whose lights convinced me that even Hollywood could not glitter as brightly.

To walk into The Arcade for the first time was to realize that architecture could be every bit as melodic and inspiring as a great song

or a Rocky Colavito round tripper.

And then it was a quick detour down East Sixth to Royal Castle for a couple of burgers and a frosted mug of birch beer. That, my friend, was living large!

The intersection of East Ninth and Euclid was the great gateway to forbidden territory. Turn south and you found yourself crossing Prospect where the walls of the pawnshops were lined with treasure the likes of which we had never seen. We lusted for the dust-covered guitars and drums, assured the bored owner that we were serious about buying, and wanted nothing more than a few minutes of communion with those magical musical tools that we were sure were the first step to fame, fortune and, more importantly, girls.

From there it was only a few steps to the legendary Record Rendezvous, where, we were all to be told years later, owner Leo Mintz and legendary local DJ Alan Freed coined the phrase "rock 'n' roll." The truth is that the phrase had been around for quite some time, but when the legend exceeds the truth, print the legend.

But if lust was really what you were after, you turned north off of Euclid and, in one short block, found yourself in front of The Roxy Burlesque, whose facade was resplendent with huge pastel-tinted photos of Tempest Storm, Virginia Bell and her "amazing 48s" and the other queens of a soon-to-be-gone art form. And, in an era when brazen

And then it was a quick detour down East Sixth to Royal Castle for a couple of burgers and a frosted mug of birch beer. That, my friend, was living large!

sexuality was not exactly a national pastime, this larger-than-life display of barely covered womanhood was all the more impressive!

And that was the beauty of it all. Downtown the men seemed to walk taller, the women seemed more beautiful and the tough guys sneered harder.

Unfortunately, it seems the future forgot to give this venerable thoroughfare an invitation. All you get to keep are the memories, and my memories of downtown burn brightly. Here's hoping we can find a way to rekindle a love affair that never should have ended.

...but when the legend exceeds the truth, print the legend.

Michael Stanley, musician and radio personality.
Photographed at WNCX in downtown Cleveland.

ruby Dee

I was born in Cuyahoga County. I say Cuyahoga County because I liked the sound of such a place better than just Cleveland. It sounded fancy, faraway and Indian, which fit in with what my brother, Edward, had told me and my younger sister, LaVerne, one day. "We're part Indian, you know. Uncle Roosevelt told me we're relatives of Sitting Bull. We're also part Irish. That's where LaVerne gets her gray eyes."

I believed him about that because just a few days before he had told LaVerne and me that our mother was not really our mother. "Your real mother's name was Gladys," he revealed with great authority. "Now, I remember Gladys. Daddy doesn't want me to talk about this, but Angelina and me have known about Gladys for a long time." LaVerne and I were stunned. We didn't believe him. We started to cry. "Don't say I told you this, but Emma is what you call a 'stepmother.'" We didn't mention this great revelation to Mother, but when Daddy came home we blabbed to him what Edward had said.

Mother heard the commotion from the kitchen – Edward trying not to cry as Daddy gave him a whipping. "I was ju-just talking to them about Cle-Cleveland, where they were born, where Angelina and me and all of us were…" Mother hurried in, wiping her hands with a dishcloth. "Stop. Stop, Ed," she interrupted. "They're bound to find out. Not his fault. We were wrong – wrong not to tell them long, long before now." She followed him from the room, talking to his back as something like grunts – mixed with sobs – escaped him.

I was almost 13 years old when my brother told me about Gladys. I had visited Cleveland a few times before then. My father, who worked as a waiter (and later as a cook) on the Pennsylvania Railroad, had taken us by train to see his brother. It was thrilling riding the train, sleeping in the Pullman car and eating in the dining car. Above all, though, Cleveland meant seeing all my aunts and uncles and cousins. My Aunt Josie had 13 children. I was fascinated by her oldest daughter, Vivian, who seemed to be always bent over, washing mounds of clothes or cooking something good in huge pots. There was Josephine, Wilbur, Helen and Waldora, and on and on. It seemed to be a happy home, though I learned later what a struggle life had been for them. So for me, Cleveland meant cousins and family reunions, food and laughter.

For all that, I had a very strange relationship with Cleveland, though I didn't understand the source of that strangeness until my brother spilled the beans. For my stepmother, Emma, Cleveland meant Gladys. It was a different time for women back then, and my stepmother felt uncomfortable having another woman in our life. So the subject of Cleveland was not really welcome in our house in Harlem.

A few weeks after Edward told us about Gladys in Cleveland, my sister and I were on a train heading out there to meet her for the very first time. I remember feeling empty, drained, as if void of all capacity for emotion. I don't remember liking or disliking her. I was like a big hole — open to receive something or to feel something because she gave birth to me. Nothing had prepared me to meet this person, my mother. I don't think my father wanted Emma to know that we were actually going to meet Gladys. He didn't want to upset Emma, who up until that time was the only mother LaVerne and I had known.

We went to her house, and I remember feeling that she wanted to please us. She bought us milk and even made a chocolate cake — but she wasn't a very good cook, so we just picked at the cake. She spoke very quickly, in an almost staccato rhythm. I remember, because I often fall into that same rhythm when I am excited or don't know what to say. Then it all started to make sense: the strange gifts from Cleveland that would arrive for us in New York, with no card; and opened letters without envelopes, with the bottoms cut off.

In the end, I remember being judgmental, blaming her for having children and then running away. At 13, I couldn't understand the circumstances that had separated us. Back then, I felt I had to choose. Gladys was my mother, and there was no getting around it. But I loved my stepmother.

Emma was college-educated, an elocutionist who had wanted to be an actress. She had also wanted to have children, but an accident with a horse had made this impossible. She married my father, who had four children, and raised them as her own. She was a disciplinarian — she made sure we children learned to speak correctly, using proper diction. But she encouraged our love for poetry and music — and later, my interest in the theater. With her support, I began studying at the American Negro Theatre in New York, which propelled me to a lifelong career in the arts.

But Cleveland was always there in the background.

I have been back quite a bit over the years, but my memories of the early days are fleeting. I wish I had paid more attention.

> **Emma and Gladys, Cleveland and Harlem, are bound together forever in me, are who I am, are the bedrock that pulses me through the eternities.**

And I wish I had gotten to know Gladys better. I wish I hadn't simply dismissed my mother for not raising us, not knowing that she couldn't. I wish I could tell her that I understand now how things like that happen in this life, how even the best people have circumstances in their life they just can't control.

I wish my stepmother could have been reassured that it was all right for me to know my mother. And I wish I could take them both in my arms today, to hug them and to reassure them that everything's okay — that I understand and love them both dearly. Emma and Gladys, Cleveland and Harlem, are bound together forever in me, are who I am, are the bedrock that pulses me through the eternities.

I don't know if they ever met. My mind's eye, however, sees them stop in some beyond-time non-place, where Cleveland and Harlem are just a snap away. They do surprise pointy fingers at each other, then rear back and laugh 'til tears fall, as Ed zooms in on that elegant train, the Silver Cloud. Their wings get a little tangled in the embrace; still, they laugh and praise — shout and cry a little, too — as they fly free.   ≈

Ruby Dee, actress, first lady of stage and screen.
Photographed at her home in New Rochelle, New York.

umberto Fedeli

I love Cleveland. It would be virtually impossible to get me out of here. It's a diverse ethnic town that has all the advantages of a major city. We have sports, the lake, a great symphony orchestra, museums and beautiful suburbs.

I especially love the topography of the Chagrin Valley — the trees, rolling hills and streams. I happen to live in Gates Mills, but we have some beautiful suburbs that surround this city. I love the seasons. Spring with the flowers blooming and, of course, summer. Fall with its many colors — even winter. Although by February and March it does seem to stay a little long. But each season has its beauty, and we see a complete change here in Cleveland.

When most people talk to me, they ask about how I built my business. Believe me, Cleveland is a good town for business. But when I think of Cleveland, I think more about the people. The relationships I have built with many of the people here. They're genuine people. People who know their nationality. They know whether they are Serbian, Slovenian, Polish, Jewish, African American, Irish or Italian — which is what I am. Other towns seem more generic, more sterile. This is a real town, with real people.

Most of all, I think about my family. I was born in Collinwood and grew up in South Euclid, and as I was growing up, I was always surrounded by my large family. We have so many cousins, too many to count. Until recently, I was blessed to have all four grandparents living. My great grandmother sang at my wedding and that is a joy that I can't really express. My children know all four of their great grandparents, and now I am building memories for them.

I remember all our family get-togethers, the warmth and the love we shared. Those are precious childhood memories. We were always celebrating someone's birthday, Holy Communion or confirmation. The hugging, the kissing, the laughing, and of course, the food. The food was everywhere, the sights and smells of all those Italian delicacies. And every season had its pastries, cakes or special pastas.

Entertaining is still a joy. We have a full-blown Italian restaurant right in our home that can seat about 100 people indoors. It's very open so you can see what people are cooking. We have hundreds of events there; most of them are charitable or civic. Many times we have a guest chef. My mother is still a chef. In fact, she still cooks for us in the office from time to time — all types of pasta, lasagna and cavatelli. She also makes a wonderful scallopine. So hospitality is something that is in our family's blood. It's something that we have all come to love. Something we all grew up with.

I took that same sense of hospitality with me as I built my insurance business. I try to convey those same values to the people who are guests in my home. In life, the secret to happiness is to love, and the essence of love is to serve. That saying has been an inspiration to me throughout my life.

> **My mother is still a chef. In fact, she still cooks for us in the office from time to time... So hospitality is something that is in our family's blood. It's something that we have all come to love. Something we all grew up with.**

I am blessed to have grown up in such a large and loving family. If *Forbes* came out with a list of the richest people in terms of their relationships with friends and family, I would be on top of that list. Certainly not financially, but I would be the luckiest in terms of my friends and family.

I guess that's what I like so much about this town — its sense of people and family. Cleveland is one of the most compassionate, generous and loving communities in all of the country. No one cares about how much you know, until they know how much you care. And Clevelanders really care.

But when I think of Cleveland, I think more about the people.

Umberto Fedeli, President and CEO of The Fedeli Group.
Photographed at his home in Gates Mills.

john Thompson

t was Bernie Kosar's rookie season when the Dawg Pound was born. I became Big Dawg that same year.

Like most anyone who grows up in Cleveland, I was turned into a Browns fan by my parents. My earliest memories are of the preseason games against Detroit that my dad used to take me to. My favorite game? The overtime playoff game against Jets — for obvious reasons. That's when the Dawg Pound really came into its own. It started to build long before that, but that's the game when we really made a difference.

It was cold and the Browns were struggling the whole game. We were down 10 points in the last three minutes, then down a touchdown with a minute and a half left on the clock. The Browns had the ball at the 17-yard line, right in front of the Pound. And we got into a shouting match with Mark Gastineau of the Jets. On second down he flipped us off and we all flipped him off back. Then, on third and 27, he hit Bernie Kosar three seconds after the play ended and we got new life on the penalty. It was the Jets' chance to put the game on ice, but we had gotten under Gastineau's skin so bad, he forgot where he was. The next play Bernie threw a bomb to Slaughter, and the place went ballistic. You could hear the people with their radios on in the Pound and Nev Chandler screaming, calling it the "Pandemonium Palace." We went on to win in double overtime. My wife Mary, who's from Brooklyn, rooted for Jets during that game. Afterwards, she became a Browns fan for life.

Mary and I were married in 1984, and that's what caused me to move into the Dawg Pound. I'd had season tickets since 1978. I used to sit in Section 17, the overhang. You could really see the field from there. But when I got married, I had to get two tickets, which was pretty hard in that section. So before the start of the '85 season, Mary and I went to seat day. You remember, you used to be able to go into the old Municipal Stadium and select any seat you wanted, as long as it wasn't tagged by a season ticket holder.

I had sat in the bleachers for an Indians' game but never for a Browns' game. As Mary and I walked down the ramps on either side of the bleachers, I realized just how intense those seats were. It was like we were walking right down the ramp and onto the field. When I got to the bottom, I saw just how close the stands were to the endzone fence. When those players made a catch at the back of the end zone, they only had a foot before they came up the hill to the fence and were in the stands.

The seats were cheaper, too. It used to cost $17.50 in Section 17, but bleacher seats were only $9 each — so I basically got two seats for what one used to cost me. There weren't too many season ticket holders in the bleachers back then. Just a few guys next to me who used to call themselves the Bleacher Creatures. They were in the section next to me. They were the guys who used to bring the doghouse with the keg in it — if you can remember those tailgate parties.

Before the 1985 season started, we went to Lakeland to watch the Browns work out. That's where we heard Minnifield, Dixon, Gross and Rodgers[SP] barking at each other and the linemen. So that's where the idea started. On the first preseason game of the season, one of the Bleacher Creatures actually bought in a dog skull that was dipped in orange paint. He even had two sticks that would make it bark. I still have no idea where he got it.

That's where I saw the dog mask on the wall. It was behind the counter along with a bunch of other masks. I remember all my friends were laughing at me, trying to figure out why I wanted a dog mask.

On the Saturday before the first home game of the season, I went down to Kamms Corners to a bar called the Choir Loft. We parked outside this costume shop Starship Earth, which was having its grand opening. Well, after throwing down a few jars at the Choir Loft, we came out all happy and decided to check out the costume shop. That's where I saw the dog mask on the wall. It was behind the counter along with a bunch of other masks. I remember all my friends were laughing at me, trying to figure out why I wanted a dog mask.

The next day, we played the St. Louis Cardinals and lost, but it was the first time the dog mask made its appearance. I've been Big Dawg ever since.

It was the Jets' chance to put the game on ice, but we had gotten under Gastineau's skin so bad, he forgot where he was.

John (Big Dawg) Thompson and Debra (The Bone Lady) Darnall,
superfans. Photographed at Cleveland Browns Stadium.

debra Darnall

When the Browns left town, I boycotted the NFL. I didn't even watch the Super Bowl. Like everyone else, I was heartbroken. But by the time the 1999 expansion draft came, I was hungry for anything having to do with my beloved Browns. That's how the whole idea of "The Bone Lady" started.

I was born in Cleveland, grew up in Bath Township and Richfield, but was living in Columbus when the Browns moved. I've moved back here since. Being in Columbus and anxiously awaiting the Browns' return, an idea popped in my head. I woke up one day and said, "I'm going to paint my car like a Browns helmet and put an eight-foot bone on top." My friends said, "No you're not. That's a Volvo. You'll ruin your car."

It was the first time that I didn't listen to anyone except that little voice inside my head. I had a guy professionally paint the car, and then I went to work on the inside. I wanted the inside to be a collage of Browns memorabilia, a true tribute to the Browns' return. So I worked on it every night. I would grab a beer, turn on the Indians game, sit in my Volvo with my glue gun and paste every kind of Browns thing I could lay my hands on to the inside of my car.

As the season started getting close, I realized I would have to establish some sort of deadline for myself or I would never get it finished. So I entered myself in a Fourth of July parade in Columbus. My family came down and we were all going to be in the parade.

The night before, I realized that I couldn't be "normal" and be in the parade, so the "Bone Lady" was born. That's when I came up with my outfit — the beehive hairdo, hooped skirt and fishnet stockings. I always say "The Bone Lady" is what happens when you drink too much beer and own a glue gun!

The most memorable part of the costume was the orange biker shorts I had on under my skirt. When the skirt was flipped up, it said "Art Sucks" on my rear. At that time I wasn't over the move, but when the Ravens won the Super Bowl I thought it was best to forgive and move on. So the shorts now sport a new message every week.

The Thursday before the first preseason game, I drove up and stopped at my cousin's restaurant on Medina Square for dinner. When I came back out, there was a message from Fox 8 TV. "We love your car. We'd love to do a story," it read.

I called them up and told them that I was staying at my sister's house in Richfield. They said they wanted to follow me as I drove into Cleveland on Friday. So they filmed me all morning long and when we were finished, I walked over to Public Square where the pep rally was going on. I was totally hounded. They put me up on stage, took lots of pictures and I was on the news that evening. But the game was tomorrow, and that was all I was excited about.

The next morning I got a call from my mother and she goes, "You better go get *The Plain Dealer*. You're on the front page in that outfit in your car."

I picked up a paper and went to the muny lot to tailgate. They took footage of me and were playing it all morning on CNN. People came to the lot, and they already knew my name. It was a surreal experience. I was just excited the Browns were back.

I totally did this for myself. It's all about my love for the Browns and having fun. All of a sudden it had become this whole big thing that I never expected. I have a lot of respect for the guys in the pound that have been doing this sort of thing forever, and I would never try to step on anyone's toes. I was a little worried when I first went down there. I thought people might be mad and I'd get my butt kicked, but I made the best friends of my life.

The sad part is, the only constant left in the game of football is the fans. With free agency and the salary cap, the game is never going to be the way it was. We're never going to have a group of guys who stay here for most of their careers. It's always going to be a revolving door. It makes me sad because years from now kids won't have any real football heroes. There won't be the emotional connection that we felt growing up with the Browns. Right now there isn't a connection to this team yet. That's why the players and coaches need to get out and meet the fans. We sell out the stadium not because of this team but because of all the Browns teams that came before.

In 1999, Visa along with the NFL and the Pro Football Hall of Fame decided to honor fans who love the game of football. Every year they pick one fan from every NFL team. They actually have an exhibit dedicated to the fans.

So in 2001 I was honored to be included in The Visa Hall of Fans as the ultimate Browns fan. That is an honor that I am very proud of. There are so many great Browns fans. Many are more deserving than I am, so I feel a responsibility to represent them well.

I woke up one day and said, "I'm going to paint my car like a Browns helmet and put an eight-foot bone on top." My friends said, "No you're not. That's a Volvo."

Also, I'm very proud to be a woman and be a Browns fan. I'm so glad that the Browns don't have cheerleaders. I hope we never do. There are a lot of women who love the game of football and know a lot about it. We're not all bimbos in midriff tops dancing on the sidelines, or bouncing up and down in a beer commercial.

Being "The Bone Lady" has been the most fun I've ever had in my life. Sometimes it's like having a second full-time job. But I wouldn't change a moment. I feel like I've been on this roller-coaster ride for the last six years. I've gotten to do so many things and it's allowed me to get involved in charity events and help put a smile on some people's faces.

That's when I came up with my outfit — the beehive hairdo, hooped skirt and fishnet stockings. I always say "The Bone Lady" is what happens when you drink too much beer and own a glue gun!

austin Carr

Whoever coined the phrase, "The Miracle of Richfield" was right on target. It was a miracle, at least for me. The sights, sounds and feelings of that season will never leave me. It was the best team I ever played on.

When I was drafted by the Cleveland Cavaliers back in 1971, a lot of people asked me why I didn't try to go to a bigger market or at least a team that was winning. But I wasn't afraid of establishing something here.

The same thing happened when I went from high school to college. I narrowed my choices down to two schools, either North Carolina or the University of Notre Dame. Notre Dame was a football school, but I tried to establish a basketball tradition there, so I wasn't in awe of trying to establish a basketball tradition here.

I had a lot of ups and downs during my career. Personally, I could have accomplished twice as much as I did accomplish had I been healthy.

My first season here, I hurt my foot, and played only about half the season. The next year, I hurt my knee, and was out until almost the end of the season. I was on and off for the next two years. Then I settled down and didn't have any more injuries for the rest of my career, until my last year when I had a knee operation — that's when I decided to retire.

The 1975-76 miracle season was the highlight, but it didn't start out so well.

We had a good finish to the 1974-75 season, missing the playoffs by one missed jump shot. Everybody was looking forward to next year. But then we started out 6 and 11, and everybody was wondering what was wrong with the Cavs. We were on a roll the year before, but we just couldn't get it together. Then we got Nate Thurmond, and it just took off. We never looked back from that point on.

It was a great year. Everywhere you went, people were into it. If we lost a game, the whole city was sad. If you went to the grocery store, the dry cleaners or the gas station, everybody would be walking with their heads down. But if we won a game, it was like New Year's Eve. For me, it was an emotional roller coaster I'll never forget.

During the games at the old Richfield Coliseum, it was impossible to hear anything but the crowd. We had to work our signals and calls with sign language, it was so loud. It affected our opponents more because they couldn't hear their signals, either. We were home, and we were such a close-knit team that it didn't matter. We always knew what was on each other's minds — we were just that close. We eventually won the Central Division title.

So everything fell into place.

We went to the playoffs and eventually made it to the Eastern Conference finals against the Celtics. We weren't underdogs, we weren't favorites — we were on a par with the Celtics. And we played them tough.

Until game six.

It was like letting the air out of a balloon. After the game, the locker room was somber because we weren't ready for the season to end. I'll never forget that feeling as long as I live. A few days afterward, we were all looking forward to the next season. And then free agency hit us. Jim Clemens left, and everything slowly started to fall apart. In 1979, the Cavs put me up for the expansion draft. They thought that because of my age, and the number of years on my contract, that no one would take me. But I was the first player taken by Dallas. I was eventually traded and wound up with the Bullets.

That's how it all unfolded, but my love affair with Cleveland and its fans was far from over. I came back as a Bullet on January 3, 1981, and they retired my jersey. My teammates were stunned. Here I was on an opposing team, it was halftime and I was watching number 34 go up into the ceiling. I can't tell you what that meant to me.

Today, I really like being an announcer. It keeps me close to the games. It keeps me involved and it keeps me close to the players. I also enjoy working with Michael Reghi because he teaches me a lot about the business. We also like each other, and I think that comes across on the air.

I think the players like me, too. Having your number in the ceiling helps a lot, but I think there is also an understanding that I am a real person. I don't have any pretenses. That makes them relax.

Whoever coined the phrase, "The Miracle of Richfield" was right on target. It was a miracle, at least for me. The sights, sounds and feelings of that season will never leave me. It was the best team I ever played on.

Cleveland has been my home since I was drafted in 1971. I never left. Back then, Cleveland was just another big Midwestern town, a lot of industry. But it was a lot bigger and a lot more exciting than South Bend.

When I first came here, I was told not to stay downtown after dark. Now people are living downtown. Cleveland has gone through something of a renaissance. It's slowed a bit in recent years along with the economy, but I'm sure it will pick back up again.

I think the Cavs are on the right track, too. And I'm not afraid to tell people what I see. I don't sugarcoat things. The franchise is pointed in the right direction. With LeBron James, his style of play just lends itself to winning, because he's a team player.

Now we have to put more guys around him who are focused on winning as a unit, instead of as individuals. That's when you'll see some more miracle seasons.

Austin Carr, Cleveland Cavaliers forward and announcer.
Photographed in the locker room at Gund Arena.

jane Scott

lvis Presley...Frank Sinatra...The Sex Pistols...Duke Ellington...The Rolling Stones...Bruce Springsteen...and even a former president of the United States and his vice president.

They don't share the same audience, but they all stayed at a former landmark in downtown Cleveland, the old Swingos Hotel.

It was not only the wild rock and roll hall of famous travelers from 1971 to the mid-'80s. It became one of the inspirations for Cameron Crowe's movie, "Almost Famous," and the hotel had a cameo appearance in that film.

Jim Swingos bought the Keg and Quarter restaurant at Euclid Avenue and East 18th Street when he was 25, then five years later, in 1971, he bought the 150-room hotel, the Downtowner, above it.

Elvis Presley stayed there when he played Cleveland, but he really wanted the hotel as a business base when he was on tours, so he rented 100 rooms.

Swingos grew up on Greek music and doo-wop, but quickly got into rock and roll. He was the only hotel head to cater to the long-haired rockers and their wild antics. He had 100 percent tolerance. He created theme rooms, like an exotic Casablanca suite and one with a big round bed that almost filled the room. Rockers never knew what to expect...not like a Holiday Inn.

Swingos never complained when they trashed a room. He knew the accountant traveling with them would pay the damage. Worst trashers? Led Zeppelin. One of their bills was $13,000.

Steve Popovich, owner of Meatloaf's label, Cleveland International Records, says it was the only place where you could get service 24 hours a day, if you requested it.

And you might have found yourself sitting next to anyone from Tom Petty to Iggy Pop in the bar, or Cher and Gene Simmons of Kiss. Not Rod Stewart, though. He loved to wander around and play and sing with local bands there. Some were booked by Joyce Halasa, who did public relations for the nearby Agora club.

President Jimmy Carter and Vice President Walter Mondale stayed there, but only for one night.

Naturally, some nights were livelier than others. I'll never forget the

Swingos never complained when they trashed a room. He knew the accountant traveling with them would pay the damage. Worst trashers? Led Zeppelin. One of their bills was $13,000.

night of The Who's media party when drummer Keith Moon showed up in an authentic police uniform and suddenly handcuffed WMMS-FM radio manager Kid Leo to an unknown blonde.

Bob Marley and the Wailers cooked their own Rastafarian dinner in their fourth-floor suite. Delicious, but sadly, Marley told me I was going to hell because I was not a Rastafarian.

The old Swingos, which closed in 1985, is now a Comfort Inn. Somehow it's not the same. ✒

It became one of the inspirations for Cameron Crowe's movie, "Almost Famous," and the hotel had a cameo appearance in that film.

Jane Scott, retired rock and roll journalist for The Plain Dealer. *Photographed at the former Swingos Hotel in Cleveland.*

tim Conway

y family moved to Chagrin Falls when I was five years old and I went to school there through the 12th grade, so my entire childhood was spent in that wonderful little village. I even love the change of season and weather in Northeast Ohio — everything except that snow and wind part. That isn't good.

But Chagrin Falls is a very pleasant town. It has a very Tom Sawyer-like quality to it. I'm not saying they're behind the rest of the country, but fortunately they are. What's beautiful is they've kept it that way. The local popcorn shop is about the biggest industry in town.

I used to come back quite often just to walk around town or visit old friends. Often I'd bring along my kids and spend summers there. And until just recently, I would stop back and visit the teachers who were extremely influential in my life. There was my high school coach Ralph Quisenberry, an English teacher named Elsa Jane Carroll, and my shop teacher, Norman Frye. You can still go to Chagrin Falls and find some people who have very fond memories of those teachers, because Chagrin Falls is a place where everybody knows everybody and everybody cares about everybody.

A lot of humor in the Midwest comes from places like Chagrin Falls. There is a genuine kind of humor in the Midwest. I drew a lot of my characters from my life and my surroundings, although I don't think I could cite a specific person.

A lot of people don't know that growing up in Chagrin Falls I was Tom Conway. I had to change my name when I joined Steve Allen's variety show because there was already another Tom Conway in the business, and you couldn't have two people in the union with the same name. But I was never crazy about Tom so Tim worked out well. It really wasn't much of a trade-off.

Back then, I really wasn't interested in theater. Believe it or not, I wanted to be a jockey. My dad trained a couple of horses at Randall and Thistledown, so I hung around the tracks a lot. Of course, being terrified of horses and falling off as much as I did, I figured being a jockey wasn't the best occupation for me.

I went into the Army in 1956, and was sent out west to defend the City of Seattle, a service I performed valiantly until 1958. We were never attacked during that time. When I came back, Jack Riley was leaving Big Wilson and going into the Army, so a friend suggested I apply for his job. So, I got my start with Biggy. He had a television show where he played the piano, and he had a canary that sang, so my job was to write a few skits and clean the bird cage — which was just a short scale up from what I was doing in the Army.

I met up with Ernie Anderson at Channel 3 and followed him over to Channel 8 as a director and producer — of course I did neither at the time, but it really didn't matter. It turned out Ernie didn't have much talent either so it worked out well.

Our show was so horrible, we couldn't book any guests. So I was the guest every day. One day I'd be a bull fighter, the next day I'd be a trumpet player — and we just showed movies and did our own thing. Till one day Rose Marie came through town promoting the "Dick Van Dyke Show," and she thought what we were doing was just hysterical. I told her we were just fighting for our lives, but she thought it was great.

The next thing I knew, I got an offer to join Steve Allen's Sunday variety show for a few spots, but when that was through I came back to Cleveland. It wasn't long before I got the offer to play Ensign Parker on "McHale's Navy," and being young and ambitious I did the smart thing: I turned them down.

I told them I was happy working in Cleveland. The station manager here caught wind of it and fired me. He said I was nuts not to take the offer. By firing me, he gave me no choice. Of course, that led to a very successful career. And I have had the good fortune to work with some of the best people in the business. People like Carol Burnett, Harvey Korman, Steve Allen, Don Knotts and Louis Nye

Our show was so horrible, we couldn't book any guests. So I was the guest every day. One day I'd be a bull fighter, the next day I'd be a trumpet player — and we just showed movies and did our own thing.

It may sound stupid, but I really did like working in Cleveland television back then. We did our own thing. There was no talk about the mechanics of television, or the financial considerations. When you needed a prop, you went down to the magic store and bought it — or you made it yourself. And if it looked homemade, it was even funnier. I loved the people I worked with here, and consider many of them lifelong friends.

But even more important, I was never far from that beautiful little village where I grew up — a place in the middle of a valley with waterfalls and a popcorn shop — a place I am proud to call home.

A lot of humor in the Midwest comes from places like Chagrin Falls.

Tim Conway, actor and comedian.
Photographed at the Stardust Casino/Hotel, Las Vegas.

louis Stokes

y brother Carl and I got interested in politics by virtue of our training as lawyers and the fact that we were born and raised in Cleveland.

We felt a very strong need to give back to the community, to utilize our educations and opportunities to reach back and help those who came up through similar circumstances, particularly those coming out of poverty, welfare and public housing, which had been our background.

I don't hesitate to tell people that I really do love Cleveland. It's one of the few cities in the United States that offers so much to families, especially people who want to raise their children in a family kind of environment. It's also a city that will permit you to be anything you want. Cleveland is a place where you can reach your full potential.

Looking back on my 30-plus years in Cleveland politics, the most exciting night was the night my brother Carl became the first black mayor of Cleveland. In winning that election, he made history by becoming the first black mayor of a major American city. Cleveland, at the time, was the eighth largest city in the United States. It had more than 800,000 people. But his election did a lot more.

It was looked upon by black Americans all over the country as a goal that they could set in their respective cities. If Carl Stokes could win in Cleveland, where the black population was only 37 percent, they too could start to look at the possibility of electing a black mayor in New York, Los Angeles, Chicago, Philadelphia and other major cities. Indeed, that's exactly what happened.

The race was tight right up until election night. By 6:30 p.m., when the polling places closed, his headquarters on Huron Road was packed with people, spilling over onto the sidewalks. The early results showed him ahead by a few points, then back even, then ahead again. It was back and forth all evening and the crowd continued to grow, spilling out onto Huron Road. We didn't know who the winner was until about three o'clock in the morning.

When the news came that Carl had won, people started dancing in the streets. A young black man ran up to me and said, "Lou, do you know what this means? It means that for the first time in my life I can look my son in the eye and tell him that you can be anything that you want to be."

"Lou, do you know what this means? It means that for the first time in my life I can look my son in the eye and tell him that you can be anything that you want to be."

Following the model Carl set in Cleveland, we did get black mayors in many major American cities including Los Angeles, New York, Chicago, Philadelphia, Baltimore and Denver. But he was the first.

Of course, my election to Congress the following year was another historic occasion because I was the first black American to ever be elected to Congress from the State of Ohio. Our state was admitted to the Union in 1803, so it was a long time coming. In fact, though I am now retired after serving in Congress for 30 years, I am still the only black male ever elected to represent Ohio in Congress.

It was a great moment for our state, and the people in Congressional District 21. But I still consider Carl's election as mayor of Cleveland as the highlight of both of our political careers.

...I was the first black American to ever be elected to Congress from the State of Ohio. Our state was admitted to the Union in 1803, so it was a long time coming.

Louis Stokes, former U.S. Congressman.
Photographed at The Capitol, Washington, D.C.

biographies

John Adams

A native Clevelander, John Adams has been pounding out support for his beloved Cleveland Indians for nearly five decades. In fact, April 2005 marks 50 continuous seasons of opening game attendance for Adams. A graduate of Parma High School, Adams went on to get a B.A. in English from Cleveland State University. He currently works as a data systems analyst for SBC. He is a resident of Brecksville.

Dr. Elizabeth K. Balraj

Considered a national leader in her field, Dr. Balraj began her work at the Cuyahoga County Coroner's office in 1972 as a pathologist. She was appointed coroner of Cuyahoga County in 1987 when Dr. Samuel R. Gerber retired. Since 1988 she has been reelected continuously to the office. During her tenure she has been involved in the investigation of more than 10,000 deaths due to violence or suspected violence. She is the first woman to be elected to the office, and is also the first coroner to be board certified in forensic pathology. In addition to her responsibilities as coroner, she has instructed students at Case Western Reserve University's School of Medicine as an assistant professor in Forensic Pathology since 1973, and is the director of the Forensic Pathology Fellowship Program at the Cuyahoga County Coroner's Office. In addition, Balraj is involved in numerous other academic affiliations and professional organizations. Born in Salem, India, she now lives in Solon with her husband.

Mike Belkin

As a concert and special events promoter, Michael Belkin has had a tremendous impact on the development of Cleveland's image as the Rock and Roll Capital of the world. Together with partner and brother Jules Belkin, Mike Belkin formed Belkin Productions in 1966 promoting a concert by The Four Freshman at Cleveland Music Hall. The Belkin brothers were responsible for helping to break national acts such as David Bowie, Roxy Music and Bruce Springsteen. The two brothers also buoyed local concert venues such as the Agora, Music Hall, and in later years the Odeon. SFX Entertainment, a division of Clear Channel Entertainment, eventually bought out Belkin Productions.

K. Michael Benz

As President and CEO of United Way Services of Cleveland since 1995, Michael Benz is responsible for the overall management of one of the largest and one of the first United Ways in the country, managing a budget of more than $5 million and a staff of more than 125. Prior to joining United Way, Benz was principal of his own firm, K. Michael Benz Inc., a consulting practice that focused on marketing, sponsorship and organizational development with local and national clients in both public and private sectors. Benz also served as director of the Rock and Roll Hall of Fame and Museum from 1992 to 1993, and was executive vice president of the Greater Cleveland Growth Association from 1980 to 1992. While there, Benz assisted with the start-up of the Council of Smaller Enterprises (COSE), a division of the Growth Association, building its membership from slightly over 100 members to more than 3,000. In addition to his career, Benz also is actively involved in numerous civic and professional organizations.

Jim Brown

In his all-too-brief NFL career, Jim Brown won eight NFL rushing titles, was named to nine Pro Bowls, earned two MVP awards, and racked up over 12,000 yards rushing. Brown played college ball at Syracuse University, where he became a starter as a sophomore, a star as a junior and an All-American as a senior. He also was considered one of the finest lacrosse players to ever take to a college field. While his career as an athlete was legendary, Brown went on to star in numerous Hollywood films, appearing in such exciting action films as "The Dirty Dozen" and "100 Rifles" and "Mars Attacks!" A controversial figure throughout his career, Brown has long been a champion of civil rights, being one of the first African-American sports figures to speak out on important issues. More recently he has worked among the gangs of Los Angeles, spreading his message of hard work, education and self respect. He is considered simply the best to have ever played the game of football.

Austin Carr

The first draft pick of the expansion Cleveland Cavaliers in 1971, Austin Carr grew up in Washington, D.C., and attended the University of Notre Dame in Indiana. He built a reputation as a scoring machine with the Fighting Irish, scoring 50 or more points in a game on nine separate occasions. In his rookie season with the Cavs, Carr averaged 21 points per game, maintaining an average of over 20 points per game for the next two years. While a knee injury cut his playing time in 1974, he remained dedicated to the Cavs, eventually playing a pivotal role in the 1975-76 playoff season that became known as the "Miracle of Richfield." In 1981 his number 34 jersey was retired. He has since been named to the All-Time Best Cleveland Cavalier team. While his career on the court is behind him, Carr is still active in the sport, working the sidelines as a Cav's commentator for away games. He still lives in Mayfield Heights with his wife Sharon. They have two grown children.

Tim Conway

Changing his name from Tom to Tim to avoid confusion with another actor, Chagrin Falls' Tim Conway has made a name for himself on television and the silver screen. Originally a regular with Big Wilson and later Ghoulardi, Conway was discovered by comedienne Rose Marie as she swung through town on a promotional tour. This led to a position as a regular on the "Steve Allen Show" for Conway. Conway went on to play the bumbling Ensign Parker on "McHale's Navy." In addition, Conway appeared in a number of family comedy romps for Disney, among them "The Apple Dumpling Gang," "The Billion Dollar Hobo," "The Prize Fighter" and "The Apple Dumpling Gang Rides Again." He starred in several video productions as a character named "Dorf," a comedic dwarf. He was also a regular on "The Carol Burnett Show," where his remarkable comedic timing, physical comedy routines and ability to keep a straight face became legendary.

Debra Darnall

Debra Darnall, aka The Bone Lady, grew up in Richfield and Bath, Ohio. Known for her outlandish faux beehive hairdo and hoop skirt costume with various Browns' slogans plastered on her burnt sienna skirt, Darnall is a fixture in the Dawg Pound of Cleveland Browns Stadium. She graduated from Revere High School in Bath and moved to Columbus where she lived for 16 years. A decorative painter, she is now a resident of Lakewood. She was the 2001 inductee for the Visa Hall of Fans at the Pro Football Hall of Fame in Canton, Ohio.

Ruby Dee

The daughter of a Pullman-porter father and a schoolteacher mother, Ruby Dee was born in Cleveland but grew up in Harlem. While in New York, she studied under Morris Carnovsky at the American Negro Theater. Her first stage success came as the title character in "Anna Lucasta." She married fellow actor Ossie Davis in 1948 and the two have starred in numerous productions, including their joint film debut in "No Way Out." Dee appeared in "The Jackie Robinson Story," playing Jackie's wife. She also played his mother years later in the made-for-television movie, "The Court-Martial of Jackie Robinson." She also has been prominently featured in the works of director Spike Lee in "Do the Right Thing" and "Jungle Fever." Other notable film credits include "Buck and the Preacher" and "A Raisin in the Sun." On television she was a regular on "The Guiding Light," "Roots: The Next Generations" and "Middle Ages." She won an Emmy for her performance in the Hallmark Hall of Fame presentation "Decoration Day" in 1990. An accomplished writer, Dee also has been a regular contributor to the *Amsterdam News*, and has penned several books including *Glowchild*, a book of poetry, *My One Good Nerve* and *With Ossie and Ruby: In This Life Together*, which she wrote with her husband Ossie Davis.

Harrison Dillard

Considered the best hurdler of his time, Dillard is the only athlete ever to win individual Olympic gold medals in a sprint and hurdle event. Initially just a hurdler, at one point in his career he won 82 consecutive races. However, in his first attempt to reach the Olympics in 1948 he hit several hurdles and failed to qualify. He qualified for the Olympics that same year by finishing third in the 100-meter dash. He later won Olympic Gold in a virtual dead heat with teammate Barney Ewell, tying the world record of 10.3 seconds. In 1952 he qualified for the 110-meter high hurdles, winning his second individual gold medal. He also won the gold medal in the 4 X 100 meter relay teams in both 1948 and 1952.

Phil Donahue

Considered a pioneer of the modern talk show format, Phil Donahue was born in Cleveland, graduated from St. Edward High School in Lakewood, and later the University of Notre Dame in South Bend, Ind. Donahue's broadcast premiere was in Dayton, Ohio, with his radio program "Conversation Piece." Two years later "The Donahue Show" appeared on television. Controversial atheist Madalyn Murray O'Hair was his first guest. Donahue starred in numerous roles throughout his career on both television and the silver screen. He has won more than 20 daytime Emmys. His latest show, "Donahue," was canceled by MSNBC. While not currently on the air, Donahue continues to be as opinionated as ever, and is still active in politics. Donahue now resides in New York with his wife, actress Marlo Thomas.

Denise Dufala

Denise Dufala first appeared on Cleveland television in 1986, and soon became a favorite with the hometown crowd. As anchor of Channel 19's "Action News," Dufala combines her strong Cleveland roots with experience in reporting and anchoring to deliver insight to local, national and world events. Dufala grew up in North Olmsted and earned a B.A. in journalism from The Ohio State University. Prior to joining "Action News," she served as the 6 p.m. and 11 p.m. news anchor at WJW-TV. Prior to that, she was the original morning anchor of "Newscenter 8 This Morning" at the same station. An Emmy-winning reporter, Dufala also finds time to donate much of her free time to charitable causes, including the Make-A-Wish Foundation. Her interests include antiques collecting, ice skating and singing. Indeed, her talent and passion for the latter finds her singing regularly in her church choir, as well as performing the National Anthem before Cleveland Indians, Browns, Cavaliers and Crunch games.

Joe Eszterhas

Born in Hungary, Eszterhas came to the United States in 1950 after spending the first six years of his life in Hungarian refugee camps. In fact, the well-known screenwriter and author has been awarded the Emanuel Foundation's Lifetime Achievement Award for his work dedicated to the memory of the holocaust in Hungary. A former reporter for *The Plain Dealer*, Eszterhas rose to national prominence for his articles in *Rolling Stone* magazine. He was a National Book Award nominee for "Charlie Simpson's Apocalypse," as well as the screenwriter of blockbusters such as "Basic Instinct" and "Jagged Edge."

Dick Feagler

Long considered the dean of Cleveland letters, Dick Feagler is a featured columnist for *The Plain Dealer*. A Cleveland native, Feagler graduated from Ohio University. After serving in the Army, and a brief stint with the *Sandusky Register*, Feagler joined the *Cleveland Press* as a general assignment reporter, later growing into a position as a column writer in 1970. His column ran in the Press from 1970 until the paper folded in 1982. Throughout the 1980s, Feagler's columns appeared in many papers in Northeast Ohio, including the *Akron Beacon Journal*, *The News-Herald*, *The Morning Journal* in Lorain and *The Chronicle-Telegram* in Elyria. He joined *The Plain Dealer* in 1993, where his columns appear to this day. In addition to his career in the print media, Feagler also has been seen in commentaries for both WKYC and WEWS, as well as hosting the popular weekend interview program "Feagler and Friends" on WVIZ — winning numerous Emmy Awards. He also served as a senior editor for *Cleveland Magazine*, and was a contributing editor of *Corporate Cleveland*. He has appeared on NBC's "Today" and Tom Snyder's "Tomorrow." Many of his commentaries have been heard on National Public Radio.

Umberto P. Fedeli

Since 1988 Umberto P. Fedeli has served as president and CEO of The Fedeli Group, one of the largest privately held insurance companies in Ohio. Under Fedeli's leadership, the company has been recognized as one of the top five privately held insurance agencies in Cleveland and has been twice named to the Weatherhead 100 list of fastest growing companies in Northeast Ohio. Committing a large amount of his time to civic and charitable causes, Fedeli is a member of the Board of Trustees for the Cleveland Clinic Foundation and John Carroll University. He also serves as chairman of the Catholic Cemeteries Association and the Northern Italian American Foundation — a charitable organization he helped found in 1995. Fedeli also is actively involved with Legatus, an international group of Catholic CEOs, serving as president of the organization's Cleveland chapter as well as on the International Board of Directors. In 1991 Fedeli was appointed by then Governor George Voinovich to head the Ohio Turnpike Commission, serving as its chairman for six years. Under his leadership, the turnpike's resources were used as a catalyst for growth and economic development. An alumnus of St. Joseph High School and John Carroll University, Fedeli resides in Gates Mills with his wife Maryellen and their five children.

Bob Feller

Born in Van Meter, Iowa, in 1918, former Indians pitcher Bob "Rapid Robert" Feller joined the Cleveland Indians in 1936. During his career he racked up more than 262 wins, 2,581 career strikeouts, 12 one-hitters and 3 no-hitters, despite losing four seasons to Naval service during World War II. Known for his blistering fastball, Feller tied a record for strikeouts in a game when he struck out 17 batters during his rookie year. Two years later he broke his own record with 18 strikeouts against the Detroit Tigers. During his time on the mound, the Indians posted some of the best seasons in the franchise's storied history, winning one World Series in 1948 in addition to two American League Pennants. The team finished second seven times. Feller left the mound for a successful business career in 1956. He was inducted into the Baseball Hall of Fame in Cooperstown, N.Y., in 1962. Feller and his wife Anne live in Gates Mills.

John J. Ferchill

John J. Ferchill, Chairman/CEO of The Ferchill Group, possesses an impressive background in virtually every aspect of real estate development. His extensive experience includes a diverse range of projects, over 40 of which he personally has directed to successful conclusions. Since its incorporation in 1978, The Ferchill Group has earned a national reputation within the competitive world of commercial real estate as a company that delivers. The company specializes in middle- and low-cost housing developments, historic restoration projects, luxury housing, and first-class commercial office and urban mixed-use projects. The company is involved in every stage of development, from concept design to construction management and on-line operations. The Ferchill Group has been involved in development projects in excess of one billion dollars. A committed civic activist, Mr. Ferchill has served as chairman of the Greater Cleveland Sports Commission and the Ohio Canal Corridor. In addition, Mr. Ferchill is active with his deceased daughter's foundation, The Jennifer Ferchill Foundation. Mr. Ferchill is a graduate of Cleveland State University, where he majored in Electrical Engineering.

Richard Gildenmeister

Considered Cleveland's best-known promoter of books for almost five decades, Richard Gildenmeister is the master bookseller at Joseph-Beth Bookseller at Legacy Village in Lyndhurst. Prior to joining that store, Gildenmeister was a master bookseller with Joseph-Beth Booksellers on Shaker Square. He also sold books for Higbee's in addition to running his own store on Shaker Square in the late 1970s. During his career he has worked with more than 9,000 writers, befriending such people as Jacqueline Suzann and Barbara Walters.

Dick Goddard

A legend in meteorological circles, Dick Goddard has served as WJW's chief meteorologist since 1966, still forecasting the weather Monday through Friday on the 5 p.m., 6 p.m. and 10 p.m. editions of FOX 8 NEWS. Goddard's initial weather training came in the 1950s during his four-year tour with the United States Air Force. During his military career he was selected to accompany the Atlantic Energy Commission on an H-Bomb detonation in the Pacific Islands. Following his discharge, he worked for five years with the Weather Bureau at the Akron-Canton Airport. During that time he attended Kent State University where he graduated in 1960 with a Bachelor of Fine Arts degree. In 1963 Goddard flew aboard a plane into the eye of "Flora," one of history's deadliest hurricanes. In a national 1987-88 survey of newscaster popularity by Herb Altman Communications Research, Goddard was rated the most popular weathercaster in America. Goddard also is known for his annual "Woollybear Festival," and has served as the football statistician for the Cleveland Browns for more than 32 years.

Dan Gray

Cleveland's best known entrepreneur, hippie and T-shirt mogul, Daffy Dan Gray is a native Clevelander who attended Shaker Heights High, where he dropped out in the last 12 weeks of his senior year because they wanted him to cut his hair. Initially operating music stores under the Melody Lane, Music Grotto and Pearl Discs names, Gray founded Daffy Dan's T-Shirt Shop in 1973 — which eventually led to more than 27 locations throughout Northeast Ohio in less than six years. Today, Gray still loves life and working in Cleveland. His dog Smedley goes to work with him every day.

Fred Griffith

Fred Griffith majored in philosophy at West Virginia University, served as an Air Force officer, and became a broadcast journalist, working as a radio news director in Charleston before moving to Cleveland in 1959. He joined WKYC after 33 years at WEWS where he held a variety of positions, including host of the two-hour "Morning Exchange" for over 26 years. Also an author and gourmand, Griffith and his wife, Linda, have been professionally involved in the world of food for over 20 years. Together they have written six books. "Nuts! The Cookbook" has just been submitted to St. Martin's Press. Their earlier works include "The Best of the Midwest" (1990, Viking), "The New American Farm Cookbook" (1993, Viking), "Onions Onions Onions" (1994, Houghton Mifflin), "Cooking Under Cover" (1996, Houghton Mifflin), and "Garlic Garlic Garlic" (1998, Houghton Mifflin). Their onion book was the winner of a James Beard Award. The couple has five children and 10 grandchildren. The Griffiths live in Cleveland Heights, with a house full of pets.

Arsenio Hall

The son of a Cleveland Baptist minister, entertainer Arsenio Hall attended Ohio University in Athens where he originally intended to study law, but switched to the communications department. He later transferred to Kent State University, where he worked his way through college with gigs at local comedy clubs. After an upward climb, Hall was hired as an opening act for entertainers such as Dionne Warwick and Nancy Wilson. He was later befriended by superstar Eddie Murphy — the two comedians starred in the 1987 film comedy "Coming to America." A favorite guest on "The Late Show Starring Joan Rivers," Hall took over as host when Rivers got the ax, heading up the "Arsenio Hall Show," a late-night entry syndicated by Paramount Television. With his trademark "Whoop, Whoop" and willingness to book cutting-edge guests, Hall quickly rose to the top of the ratings. In June 1990, *TV Guide* selected Hall as the magazine's first "TV Person of the Year." After five years, Hall and Paramount Television parted ways. Hall kept a low profile, all but disappearing from view until 1997. Emerging from his self-imposed exile, he has gone on to star on television and in feature films, and has been a frequent guest on "Jay Leno's Tonight Show."

Patricia Heaton

A talented actress whose career spans television, theater and film, Patricia Heaton has been honored with two consecutive Emmy awards for Outstanding Lead Actress in a Comedy Series for her portrayal as Debra Barone on CBS' top-rated series, "Everybody Loves Raymond." Heaton's first book, *Motherhood and Hollywood*, is a collection of essays chronicling her childhood, her years of struggle as an aspiring actress and how she balances her career and family with her current success on a wildly popular series. Portions of it appear in this book. Heaton recently starred in the TNT/Neil Simon production of "The Goodbye Girl." Heaton's television credits include roles on "Room for Two," "Someone Like Me," "Women of the House," and the critically acclaimed "thirtysomething." She also starred in the television movie "Miracle in the Woods" with Della Reese and appeared in the CBS movie, "A Town Without Christmas." Heaton's feature credits include "Memoirs of an Invisible Man," "Beethoven," "New Age" and "Space Jam." Heaton is married with four sons and resides in Los Angeles with her husband, actor/producer David Hunt. They have created a new production company, "FourBoys Films." Heaton is also the honorary chairperson of Feminists for Life, and a board member for the Edgemar Center for the Arts.

Marlin Kaplan

Chef Marlin Kaplan is best known for his restaurant One Walnut, the latest from the talented chef who has been in Cleveland since 1991. Kaplan actually started out in advertising shortly after graduating from NYU in 1978. A native New Yorker, he climbed the corporate ladder until he decided to forgo his career for a chance to display some creativity in the kitchen. In 1990 Kaplan accepted a position as sous chef at Sfuzzi, where he further honed his skills. A year later he was asked to oversee the restructuring of Sfuzzi in Tower City in Cleveland. Kaplan quickly established himself as a serious contender among the city's culinary set. Kaplan soon opened his first restaurant, Marlin, in 1993. He followed up by opening two more restaurants, Pig Heaven and Lira in 1996 and 1997 respectively. Since opening in 1999, One Walnut has received rave reviews for its food, wine and ambiance and has been embraced by the city of Cleveland. Kaplan's talent also has been well recognized both locally and nationally and is often given credit for boosting Cleveland's dining reputation. He has been a featured chef at the prestigious James Beard House in New York and is currently serving as a celebrity chef for the Cheese Advisory Panel. In addition, One Walnut has been included in *Gourmet* magazine's best restaurants in America for two consecutive years. In Cleveland, chef Kaplan serves as an on-air personality for a local television station and for PBS.

John Lanigan

Considered to be the dean of Cleveland radio, John Lanigan grew up in the small town of Ogallala, Neb. He worked in several major markets across the Midwest and West before moving to Cleveland in 1970 to join WGAR. He joined WMJI in 1985, and his morning show was soon the highest-rated daily broadcast in Ohio. Currently the host of the "Lanigan and Malone Show," Lanigan's controversial style and conservative views are considered the cutting edge of Cleveland radio. Sometimes he is described by critics as offensive, but good or bad, people listen. On his current show, Lanigan features current events, celebrity interviews and daily contests. He prides himself on the fact that the "Lanigan and Malone Show" is often an open forum for the public to voice its opinion.

Kid Leo

Anyone growing up in Cleveland in the 1970s knows the soothing velvet voice of Kid Leo, the man who made WMMS one of the premier rock-and-roll radio stations in the nation. After graduating from Cleveland State University, Kid Leo (Lawrence J. Travagliante) joined the station in 1973, after it had been on the air five years. Within three years Kid Leo had taken the station to the top of the ratings in the Cleveland area. His belief in rock and roll, an irreverent attitude and an uncanny knack for recognizing new and upcoming rock-and-roll acts propelled WMMS to the forefront of the radio industry, while helping Cleveland garner the moniker, The Rock and Roll Capital of the World. He currently lives in New York just outside of New York City, where his voice can still be heard on the airwaves.

Floyd D. Loop, M.D.

The son of an Indiana country doctor, Dr. Floyd D. Loop graduated from Purdue University in 1958 and received his M.D. from The George Washington University, Washington, D.C. His postgraduate surgical training included appointments at The George Washington University, The U.S. Air Force at Andrews Air Force Base and at the Cleveland Clinic Foundation. Loop joined the Department of Thoracic and Cardiovascular Surgery of the Cleveland Clinic in 1970 and was named chairman of the department in 1975, serving in that capacity for 14 years until his appointment as CEO and Chairman of the Board of Governors of Cleveland Clinic. Having an international reputation as a skilled thoracic and cardiovascular surgeon, Loop and his colleagues at the Cleveland

Clinic are responsible for many surgical innovations, including today's widespread use of arterial conduits in coronary artery surgery, innovations in valve repair and technical improvements in re-operations, many of which they pioneered. During his career as a surgeon, Loop performed more than 12,000 open-heart procedures and is the author of more than 350 articles on all aspects of cardiovascular surgery. He has served on the editorial boards of numerous periodicals and also has been a guest lecturer at many cardiology and surgical meetings. Loop has won numerous awards throughout his career for his dedication to both the medical profession and civic matters. He recently retired from his post as CEO and Chairman of the Board of Governors of Cleveland Clinic.

Alex Machaskee

As Publisher, President and CEO of *The Plain Dealer*, Alex Machaskee is responsible for the publication and distribution of Ohio's largest daily newspaper. Born in Warren, Ohio, Machaskee worked as a sports reporter and general assignment reporter for the *Warren Tribune* prior to joining *The Plain Dealer* in 1960. After serving as vice president and general manager, Machaskee was named publisher of the paper in 1990. Long active in Cleveland's civic scene, Machaskee has demonstrated leadership and commitment to the community throughout his career. He was recently honored by the Greater Cleveland Urban League with the Whitney M. Young Humanitarian Award and has been named International Business Executive of the Year by the World Trade Center of Cleveland, in addition to numerous other accolades and awards. He was inducted into the Northeast Ohio Business Hall of Fame in 2001. Machaskee graduated from Cleveland State where he received a B.A. in marketing. He also received an honorary Doctor of Humane Letters from CSU and the University of Akron.

Adele Ryan Malley

Recently retired after heading up Malley's Chocolates, Cleveland's premier chocolatier Adele Ryan Malley was born in Cleveland and grew up in Fairview Park. She is a graduate of St. Augustine Academy and Immaculate Jr. College, in Washington, D.C. She also took classes in teaching at John Roberts Powers in New York. After growing up in her own family business, she married Bill Malley in 1959 and joined him in the candy business. Her lilting voice can still be heard on Malley's advertisements — almost making you taste the chocolates just by her description. She made Malley's chocolate-covered strawberries a Cleveland staple. Bill and Adele Malley have six children, three in the business and three pursuing other careers.

Jenni Meno

While she considers Westlake her hometown, Jenni Meno was born in Chicago and lived in Columbus before moving to Lakewood when she was 10 years old, later moving to Westlake. A graduate of Westlake High School, Meno began pair skating with husband Todd Sand, starting their careers on a positive note by placing fifth at the first World Championships in 1993. The pair went on to the 1994 Olympics and the 1995 and 1996 World Championships where they won bronze medals. After a strong showing in the 1998 Olympics, the pair took a silver medal at the World Championships that same year. Today, the pair is professional, touring with Stars on Ice. The couple makes their home in Thousand Oaks, Calif., but gets back to Westlake on a regular basis.

Samuel H. Miller

As an entrepreneur, businessman and philanthropist, Sam Miller is certainly no stranger to Cleveland's business and civic scene. A graduate of Harvard Business School in 1943 with an M.B.A. Phi Beta Kappa, Miller attended Case Western Reserve University where he graduated in 1941. From 1947 until the present time, he has served with Forest City Enterprises Inc., most recently as its Co-Chairman of the Board and Treasurer. In addition, he has served on the Board of Trustees for Cleveland State University, the Catholic Diocese of Cleveland Foundation, Medical Mutual of Ohio, the Police Memorial, Crimestoppers, Baldwin-Wallace College, WVIZ-TV25, and Jewish National Fund. He is also National Chairman of the United Jewish Appeal and on the Honorary Lifetime Board of Trustees of the Jewish Community Federation of Cleveland. He has been the recipient of numerous civic and professional awards throughout his career.

A. Malachi Mixon III

As Chairman of the Board and CEO, Malachi Mixon has led Invacare Corp. since he led a leveraged buyout of the company in 1979. A highly regarded businessman and entrepreneur, Mixon serves on the boards of several Cleveland area corporations and civic organizations and has been an active investor in the start-up or rebuilding of several area companies. He also has been recognized nationally for his business skills and leadership. The awards and accolades Mixon has accumulated during his career are simply too lengthy to begin to list here. Mixon received his M.B.A. from Harvard, after serving four years with the United States Marine Corps, including a year in Vietnam. He attained the rank of Captain with combat decorations that include the Air Medal with Oak Leaf Cluster and the Navy Commendation Medal with a Combat V.

The Rev. Dr. Otis Moss Jr.

Pastor of the Olivet Baptist Church in Cleveland since 1975, Dr. Moss has over 35 years of direct involvement with the Civil Rights Movement. Before joining Olivet Baptist Church, Moss co-pastored Ebenezer Baptist Church in Atlanta, a church that had been pastored by Dr. Martin Luther King Jr. He currently serves as Chairman of the Board of Trustees of Morehouse College, the alma mater of Martin Luther King Jr. Moss has traveled widely and is in high demand as a lecturer and preacher. He was selected by *Ebony* magazine as one of the 10 most influential preachers in America.

Mary Rose Oakar

A lifelong resident of Cleveland's historic Ohio City neighborhood, Mary Rose Oakar has served in legislative branches of government at the local, state and national level. She was a member of Cleveland City Council from 1974 to 1976, a Congresswoman from 1977 to 1993, and a member of the Ohio House of Representatives from 2001 to 2003. She was also an educator, working as a lay teacher at Lourdes Academy and a college professor at Cuyahoga Community College, as well as other college institutions. She also has dedicated her time to teaching in an Elders Program at Cuyahoga Community College in Cleveland. During her career in Congress, she was recognized for her commitment to the elderly when she received The Excellence in Public Service Award from The Alliance for Aging Research and The Claude D. Pepper Award for Work on Aging Issues from The National Association for Homecare. She also was appointed by President Clinton to be a part of the 25-member advisory board for the White House conference on aging. In 1993 she became CEO and President of Mary Rose Oakar & Associates Inc., a position that she continues to hold.

Harvey Pekar

Cleveland native Pekar is best known for his autobiographical, slide-of-life comic book series "American Splendor," which was recently made into a movie. The comic book series, published on an approximate annual basis since 1976, chronicles Pekar's downtrodden life. The series was self-published until the early 1990s when Dark Horse took over publication. In 1987 Pekar was awarded the American Book Award for the series. "American Splendor" features the illustrations of high-profile comic book artists such as Frank Stack, Joe Sacco and Robert Crumb. Pekar began his writing career as a prolific music and book critic. His reviews have been published in the *Boston Herald, The Austin Chronicle, Jazz Times, Urban Dialect,* and *Down Beat Magazine* among other journals. He has won numerous awards for both his writing and his work on public radio. Pekar and his wife Joyce Brabner also collaborated on a book-length autobiographical comic, *Our Cancer Year*. They both still live in Cleveland and are the proud guardians of girl named Danielle.

Bishop Anthony M. Pilla

The ninth Bishop of the Catholic Dioceses of Cleveland, Bishop Anthony M. Pilla attended Parkwood Elementary School and Patrick Henry Junior High School before attending Cathedral Latin. Bishop Pilla later transferred to St. Gregory High School Seminary in Cincinnati, and in 1953 came home to Borromeo College and St. Mary Seminary in Cleveland. He was ordained to the priesthood on May 23, 1953. Bishop Pilla received a Bachelor of Fine Arts in philosophy and a Master of Arts in history from John Carroll University. He also has an honorary Doctorate of Divinity from Baldwin-Wallace College, as well as an honorary Doctorate of Human Letters from Ursuline College, John Carroll University, Cleveland State University and Notre Dame College. Pope John Paul II announced his choice as Auxiliary Bishop in 1980, and in 1981 Anthony Pilla was named Ninth Bishop of

Cleveland. In 1995 Bishop Pilla was elected to the position of president of the National Conference of Bishops, where he served a three-year term representing the bishops of the United States — spiritual leaders of over 65 million Roman Catholics.

Richard W. Pogue

Now a senior advisor to corporate public relations and investor relations firm Dix & Eaton, Richard "Dick" Pogue is a recognized business and civic leader in Northeast Ohio. A retired partner of Jones, Day, Revis and Pogue, Cleveland's largest law firm, Pogue has had a distinguished legal and professional career that included growing Jones Day from a firm with 335 lawyers to 1,225 lawyers, and from five domestic offices to 20 worldwide offices. Pogue joined the firm in 1957, retiring in 1994. Pogue graduated from Cornell University and went onto law school and the University of Michigan, where he earned his Juris Doctor in 1953. From 1954 to 1957 he served as First Lieutenant, Patents Division of The Judge Advocate General, Department of the Army (Pentagon), leaving with the rank of captain. He serves on the Boards of Trustees of numerous organizations and maintains very active civic involvement to this very day.

William Preucil

William Preucil became concertmaster of The Cleveland Orchestra April 1995 and has appeared regularly as a soloist with the Orchestra in concert performances at both Severance Hall and Blossom Music Center. His most recent appearance as soloist with the Orchestra was in March 2003. Prior to joining The Cleveland Orchestra, Preucil served for seven seasons as first violinist of the Grammy-winning Cleveland Quartet, performing more than 100 concerts each year in the world's major music capitals. From 1982 to 1989, Preucil served as concertmaster of the Atlanta Symphony Orchestra, after earlier holding the same position with the orchestras of Utah and Nashville. During his tenure in Atlanta, he appeared with the Atlanta Symphony as soloist in 70 performances of 15 different concertos. Composer Stephen Paulus's *Violin Concerto* was written for, and dedicated to, Preucil, who premiered it and then recorded it for New World Records with the Atlanta Symphony and conductor Robert Shaw. Preucil also has made solo appearances with the symphony orchestras of Minnesota, Detroit, Rochester, Hong Kong, and Taipei. Preucil regularly performs chamber music, as a guest soloist with other orchestras and at summer music festivals. Each summer he serves as concertmaster and violin soloist with the Mainly Mozart Festival Orchestra in San Diego. Preucil also continues to perform as a member of the Lanier Trio, whose recording of the complete Dvorak piano trios was honored as one of *Time* magazine's top 10 compact discs for 1993. Preucil is Distinguished Professor of Violin at the Cleveland Institute of Music and Artist in Residence at the University of Maryland School of Music. He is a Global Music Network Artist on the GMN Website and a member of the artistic advisory board for the Interlochen Center for the Arts in Michigan. He previously taught at the Eastman School of Music and at the University of Georgia. Preucil began studying violin at the age of five with his mother, Doris Preucil, a pioneer in Suzuki violin instruction in the United States. At 16 he graduated with honors from the Interlochen Arts Academy and entered Indiana University to study with Josef Gingold. He was awarded a performer's certificate at Indiana University and also studied with Zino Francescatti and Gyorgy Sebok.

Katharine Lee Reid

The director of The Cleveland Museum of Art since March 2000, Katharine Lee Reid has a special interest in 17th-century European paintings, 20th-century paintings and sculpture and late 19th- and 20th-century American and European decorative arts. Prior to joining The Cleveland Museum of Art, Reid was director of the Virginia Museum of Fine Arts, a position she held since 1991. A native Clevelander, she also served as deputy director of the Art Institute of Chicago, serving previously as that museum's assistant director. During her career, Reid also held numerous curatorial staff positions at the Ackland Art Museum at the University of North Carolina at Chapel Hill, the David and Alfred Smart Museum at the University of Chicago, and the Toledo Museum of Art in Toledo, Ohio. Reid is a magna cum laude graduate of Vassar College in Poughkeepsie, N.Y., and was awarded a master of fine arts degree from Harvard University in Cambridge, Mass.

Jack Riley

Jack Riley got his start on Cleveland radio as a sidekick to Big Wilson. From there he went on to fame as one of America's most beloved character actors, making a name for himself as Elliot Carlin, an insecure, yet hostile patient on "The Bob Newhart Show." Currently the voice of Stu Pickles of Rugrats fame, Riley also has appeared in television shows such as "Seinfeld," "The Drew Carey Show," "Touched by an Angel," "Night Court," "Alf" and "St. Elsewhere," to name a few. He also has starred in numerous movies including "Spaceballs," "The History of the World: Part One," and "Silent Movie." The co-host of "The Baxter & Riley Show" on WERE in Cleveland for more than five years, Riley has been inducted into the Ohio Broadcast Hall of Fame.

Al Roker

Seen by millions of viewers each day on NBC's top-rated "Today," Roker has a special place in his heart for Cleveland. He grew up in Brooklyn and Queens, N.Y., and attended SUNY in Oswego, N.Y., where he learned all about lake-effect snow. He began his broadcasting career in college as a weekend weatherman at WTVH TV in Syracuse, N.Y. He made a stop in Washington, D.C., before joining Channel 3 in Cleveland in 1983, his first Top 10 market. In addition to his daily appearance on NBC's "Today," Roker is also an avid writer and a producer, producing television shows for both Food TV and Court TV. He has penned several books including *Don't Make Me Stop This Car! Adventures in Fatherhood*, and is considered by many to be America's most beloved weatherman.

Sam Rutigliano

As Vice President and head coach of the Cleveland Browns from 1974 to 1984, Sam Rutigliano built a reputation for understanding players' problems as well as delivering an exciting brand of football that included numerous come-from-behind victories. He was NFL Coach of the Year in both 1979 and 1980 and led the Browns to the playoffs in 1980 and 1982. While with the Browns, Rutigliano was selected by NFL coaches to assist in developing a league-wide drug and alcohol prevention program through the NFL's Player's Association and the NFL's Management Council. Prior to joining the Browns, Rutigliano served as assistant coach with the Denver Broncos, New England Patriots and New Orleans Saints. He also was offensive coordinator at the University of Maryland and University of Connecticut. In the nascent stages of his career, Rutigliano served as Head Football Coach at Lafayette High School in Brooklyn, N.Y., and Greenwich High School in Greenwich, Conn. He also was head coach and Director of Physical Education and Athletics at Horace Greeley High School in Chappaqua, N.Y. In addition to his coaching career, Rutigliano also has been a television football analyst for NBC and author of the book *Pressure*.

Helga Sandburg

The youngest daughter of American poet Carl Sandburg, Helga Sandburg is an accomplished writer, novelist, lecturer and poet. For her writing she has won awards too numerous to list here. Her novels include, *The Wheel of Earth, Measure My Love, The Owl's Roost* and *The Wizard's Child*. Poetry collections include *The Unicorns* and *To a New Husband*. She also penned several nonfiction books including *Above and Below*, a book that explores our National Underwater Parks which she co-authored with her husband and former director of general surgery at Cleveland Clinic, Dr. George "Barney" Crile Jr. Other nonfiction works include *A Great and Glorious Romance: The Story of Carl Sandburg and Lilian Steichen*, and *...Where Love Begins*, a portrait of Carl Sandburg seen through her eyes. Her work also includes *Sweet Music*, a book of reminiscence and song and a collection of short stories entitled *Children and Lovers: Fifteen Stories*.

Chuck Schodowski

As familiar to Clevelanders as pierogis and kielbasa, "Big Chuck" Schodowski has been hosting a television show since 1966, making him the longest running local television show host. Currently seen on "The Big Chuck and Li'l John Show," Schodowski has been working in television since 1960, making his first appearance on the air when WJW launched "Shock Theater" in 1963, which was then hosted by the infamous Ghoulardi. In 1966, when Ernie Anderson retired his Ghoulardi character, Schodowski teamed up with Bob "Houlihan" Wells, co-hosting the "Big Chuck and Houlihan Show." When Wells left for Florida in 1979, "Li'l John" Rinaldi stepped into Wells' vacant co-host slot and Big Chuck and Li'l John have been popular fixture on Cleveland's late night movie scene ever since.

Viktor Schreckengost

One of the last surviving figures from the first age of Industrial Design, Viktor Schreckengost has a career in both fine arts and industrial design that spans more than 75 years. While known for his design of bicycles, pedal cars, dinnerware and pottery, Schreckengost's work in fine art has appeared in museums throughout the world, including The Metropolitan Museum of Art in New York, the Virginia Museum of Fine Art and the Cleveland Museum of Art among some 40 other museums. He also has had special exhibitions in museums throughout America and Europe and has won numerous awards for both his design and fine art. In addition to his extensive work as a designer and artist, Schreckengost also taught at the Cleveland Institute of Art, heading up that organization's industrial design program until the mid-'80s. During World War II, he served in the Navy, working in experiments with voice recognition, developing a program for radar recognition, and created new techniques for developing topographical maps using aerial photography. Schreckengost and his wife Gene still live in Cleveland Heights.

Herb Score

When he came to the Cleveland Indians as a rookie pitcher in 1955, Herb Score won an astonishing 16 games. In 1956 Score upped his strikeouts to 263, posting 20 wins, pitching a league leading five shutouts and holding opposition batters to a paltry .186 batting average. On May 7, 1957, Gil McDougald hit a line drive that struck Score in the eye, ending his season. Score made a comeback in 1958, and pitched a full season in 1959, still retaining a fine ratio of strikeouts to innings pitched. No longer unhittable, Score was traded to the Chicago White Sox where he pitched until 1962 when he retired. He became the voice of the Cleveland Indians in 1964 and had a successful play-by-play broadcast career that spanned more than three decades and saw the Cleveland Indians return to dominance at Jacobs Field.

Jane Scott

Considered a true pioneer of rock-and-roll journalism, Jane Scott has entertained readers of *The Plain Dealer* for years with her concert reviews and insight into life back stage at rock concerts. Now retired, Scott started her career at a tiny paper in Chagrin Falls in the late 1940s, finally landing a job at *The Plain Dealer* in the 1950s. Assigned to mostly obscure filler pieces, her first major break came in the form of the assignment in 1964 to cover the Beatles. They took a liking to her, inviting her back stage. Her subsequent story made the first page. Since then, Scott has been considered Cleveland's top rock-and-roll journalist, befriending the likes of Jim Morrison, Jimi Hendrix, Alice Cooper and Bob Dylan in addition to two generations of rock stars.

Molly Shannon

Born in Shaker Heights, Ohio, Molly Shannon was just 4 years old when she was in a car crash that killed her 34-year-old mother, 3-year-old sister and a 25-year-old cousin. She graduated from St. Dominic's School in Shaker Heights, went on to Hawken School and later graduated from NYU with a Bachelor of Fine Arts from NYU's Tisch School of Fine Arts. After a few small parts on television and commercials, Shannon got her big break on "Saturday Night Live," where she was a cast member from 1995 to 2001. She has since been a regular on late-night talk shows and has done numerous appearances on hit television shows such as "Seinfeld" and "Will & Grace." Shannon has also starred in numerous film roles, including the role of Mary Katherine Gallagher, which she created on SNL and which became the lead character in the 1999 hit movie "Superstar." She also recently appeared in the movie "Mean Girls."

Sister Juanita Shealey, CSJ

A native of Cleveland, Sister Juanita Shealey is the daughter of Nell Mary and Augustus Shealey. Sister Shealey's primary and high school education was entrusted to the Sisters of the Blessed Sacrament and the Society of the Precious Blood. Her college and university training was gained at an enriching number of universities and colleges, which include Case Western Reserve University, St. John's College, Dartmouth and The University of Ibadan in Nigeria, West Africa. Sister Shealey has degrees and certificates in a number of disciplines. She has a B.A. in education from St. John's College and an M.S. in guidance and counseling from Kent State University, certificates in Black History, Art and Culture from the University of Ibadan in Nigeria, West Africa, and CSU. Sister Shealey is a five-time award winner of Toastmasters International. She has lectured and designed workshops locally and nationally.

For over 20 years she has appeared twice daily on TV8 Meditations, a sign on/sign off program. She currently hosts a twice weekly inspirational radio call-in show, called "God's Saving Word" on WERE 1300.

Linn "Barnaby" Sheldon

A magical children's television entertainer for more than 32 years, Linn Sheldon is also a night club actor, comedian and storyteller. He grew up in Norwalk, Ohio, and first came onto Cleveland television sets as Barnaby in 1956, retiring in 1988. Before he was Barnaby, Sheldon was on 23 other television shows in a career that spanned more than 42 years. As Barnaby, Sheldon was famous for his spontaneous improvisational style, often making up characters out of thin air using only props. One character, Longjohn the Invisible Parrot, was his sidekick and foil for much of his time while on the air. Another sidekick, (this one real) Clay Conroy, went on to host his own show as Woodrow the Woodsman. Sheldon and his wife reside in Lakewood.

Ray Shepardson

The founder of the Playhouse Square Association and the Playhouse Square Foundation, Ray Shepardson currently works as a preservationist and restoration consultant for historic theatres across the United States. Known for re-opening theatres despite obstacles, Shepardson was born in Monroe, Wash., 40 miles northeast of Seattle, on January 13, 1944, during one of the largest snowstorms ever to hit the area. He graduated from Seattle Pacific College in 1968 with a Bachelor of Science degree in sociology and anthropology. He came to Cleveland that same year as a special assistant to Cleveland School Board President Paul Briggs. He also directed the Visiting Scholars program for the district. He founded the Playhouse Square Association in 1970, and has been working in restoration ever since. In addition to his restoration work, Shepardson is also a theatre consultant, lighting designer, producer and presenter.

Brian Sipe

Considered the most productive quarterback in Cleveland Browns history, Brian Sipe led the famed "Kardiac Kids" of the late '70s and early '80s. Known for his great comeback victories and overcoming seemingly insurmountable odds, Sipe is remembered for the 1980 season when he threw for 4,132 yards and 30 touchdowns, leading the Browns into the playoffs. He was named consensus NFL Most Valuable Player that same year. He also was elected to play in the Pro Bowl in 1981. During his career, Sipe set an individual game record for the Browns with 444 passing yards on Oct. 25, 1981, against the Baltimore Colts. He also set records for Browns career passing (23,713), touchdowns (154), attempts (3,439) and completions (1,944). Despite leading the NCAA in passing in 1971, Sipe was a 13th round draft choice of the Browns in 1972.

Michael Stanley

Born on March 25, 1948, Michael Stanley has been seriously involved with Cleveland's rock 'n' roll scene since 1965, when he formed his first band, the "Scepters." Stanley later joined the "Tree Stumps," a band that released a single, "Listen to Love." The band eventually evolved into "Silk," a locally popular group that advanced into the recording studio and produced an LP "Smooth As Raw Silk." Stanley soon produced two LPs, "Michael Stanley" and "Friends and Legends." Then in 1973, the Michael Stanley Band (MSB) came into being. From the mid '70s to the mid '80s, the Michael Stanley Band enjoyed a strong following among rock fans, touring with the likes of Bruce Springsteen, The Eagles, Foreigner and The Doobie Brothers. The band produced several top-40 hits including "He Can't Love You" in 1980 and "My Town" in 1983. In 1987 Stanley took a self-imposed hiatus from performing. The post-MSB years found Stanley still working in the Cleveland-area entertainment spotlight: He served as co-host of WJW-Channel 8's "Cleveland Tonight" and "P.M. Magazine," until they were canceled, and later as a weekly featured reporter for TV8's "First Look." But rock was never far away from his heart. He overlapped his television career with a new one in radio broadcasting — as afternoon disc jockey and on-air personality at Cleveland's WNCX 98.5. Today, Stanley continues to man the airwaves as afternoon drive-time personality at Cleveland's popular WNCX, while performing with "The Resonators" and "Midlife Chryslers" throughout Ohio.

biographies

George Stephanopoulos

George Stephanopoulos, a graduate of Orange High School, is the anchor of ABC News' "This Week," a position he has held since June 2002. Prior to being named anchor, Stephanopoulos was an ABC News correspondent, reporting on a wide variety of political, domestic and international stories for "This Week," "World News Tonight," "Good Morning America" and other ABC News programs and special event broadcasts. He also is the author of *All Too Human*, a No. 1 *New York Times* best seller on President Clinton's first term and the 1992 and 1996 Clinton/Gore campaigns. Portions of that book appear in "Cleveland Classics." Prior to joining ABC News, Stephanopoulos served in the Clinton administration as the senior advisor to the president for policy and strategy. He was a key strategist in both Clinton presidential campaigns and was involved in the development of virtually all major policy initiatives during Clinton's first term in office. During the 1992 presidential election, Stephanopoulos served on the Clinton/Gore campaign as the deputy campaign manager and director of communications. Before joining Clinton's campaign, Stephanopoulos was executive floor manager to House Majority Leader Richard A. Gephardt. Stephanopoulos received his master's degree in theology at Balliol College, Oxford University, England, where he studied as a Rhodes scholar. He holds a Bachelor of Arts degree from Columbia University and graduated summa cum laude in political science.

Terry Stewart

Terry Stewart, the president and CEO of the Rock and Roll Hall of Fame and Museum, was born and raised in Daphne, Ala., just outside Mobile. Stewart earned a Bachelor's of Science in engineering and a Bachelor's of Arts in education from Rutgers University in New Jersey in 1969. Then in 1972 and 1974, he went on to earn his M.B.A. in finance and Juris Doctor in Law at Cornell University. Stewart spent the next 15 years building a traditional business background. He served as an officer of Connecticut Bank & Trust Company from 1974 to 1979. From 1979 to 1984, he served first as vice president of business development and later as general manager of strategic planning and business development for the Continental Group Inc. From 1984 to 1989 he served as vice president of business development for Combustion Engineering Inc. Stewart then switched gears and began pursuing a career in a less traditional industry. In 1989 he joined Marvel Entertainment Group, a leader in the fields of publishing, merchandising, advertising, trading cards, toys, software and children's television. During his nine years at Marvel, he served as president and chief operating officer and later as vice chairman. Long active in civic endeavors, Stewart has served on the Boards of the U.S. Committee for UNICEF and the National Committee for the Prevention of Child Abuse. Locally, he serves on the Boards for the Cleveland Convention & Visitors Bureau, the National Conference for Community and Justice, and the Downtown Cleveland Partnership.

Louis Stokes

A distinguished congressman, lawyer and lecturer, Louis Stokes was born in Cleveland on Feb. 23, 1925. He served in the United States Army during World War II and went on to Western Reserve University and Cleveland Marshall Law School. He was the first African-American from Ohio to be elected to Congress, taking his seat from the 21st District on Jan. 3, 1969. Over the next few years he served on numerous committees, including the Committee of Official Conduct and the Permanent Select Committee on Intelligence. When Congress established the House Select Committee on Assassinations to investigate the circumstances surrounding the deaths of John F. Kennedy and Martin Luther King Jr. in September 1976, Stokes was named chairman of the committee. In 1979 the House Select Committee on Assassination reported that there was "a high possibility that two gunmen fired at president John F. Kennedy" in Dallas. Stokes retired from Congress in 1998.

Ron Sweed

Although he first made his television debut as The Ghoul in March 1971, Ron Sweed grew up in television, serving as an assistant to Ernie Anderson (Ghoulardi) when he was only 13 years old. When Ghoulardi left town in 1966, so did Sweed — to attend Bowling Green University. During that same time frame he co-produced "The Big Chuck and Houlihan Show" from 1967 to 1969. After a four-week trial run on Channel 61 in 1971 the Ghoul broke from his dead-on Ghoulardi

impersonation into a more intense, 1970s style character, using roller-skates and firecrackers on the air while showing bloody, gory, schlocky B-movies augmented with sometimes disgusting, but always funny, sound effects. Sweed continues to appear both on radio and television in Cleveland and Detroit.

John Thompson

Considered among the most rabid Browns fans, John Thompson, aka Big Dawg, can be seen in Cleveland Browns Stadium's Dawg Pound every home game wearing his trademark Dawg mask and number 98 jersey. A graduate of North Olmsted High School, Thompson is now a sales professional living in Cleveland. In 1999 Thompson was inducted to the Visa Hall of Fans at the Pro Football Hall of Fame in Canton, Ohio.

George Voinovich

U.S. Senator George Voinovich has a distinguished political career that spans nearly four decades He served as a member of the Ohio House of Representatives from 1967 to 1971; was Auditor of Cuyahoga County from 1971 to 1976 and Commissioner of Cuyahoga County from 1977 to 1978. While serving as Lieutenant Governor in 1979, Cleveland became the first major city in the U.S. to declare bankruptcy and local civic leaders urged Senator Voinovich to come back to his hometown and run for Mayor of the City of Cleveland. He was elected and served in that capacity until 1988. Under his administration the City of Cleveland underwent a dramatic turnaround. He served as Governor of Ohio from 1989 to 1998. Under the Voinovich administration, Ohio's unemployment rate fell to a 25-year low. The state created more than 500,000 new jobs and was ranked first in the nation by *Site Selection Magazine* for new and expanding business facilities. He was elected to the U.S. Senate in 1999, a position he holds to this day. Throughout his career in service to the people of Ohio, Senator Voinovich has tried to make government "work harder and smarter and do more with less." Senator Voinovich and his wife Janet still live in the same neighborhood where they first moved after they were married in 1962. They live in same house they bought in 1972.

Margaret W. Wong

Over the last 20 years Margaret Wong has built her company, Margaret W. Wong Associates Co., L.P.A., into a nationally and internationally recognized law firm that specializes in immigration and nationality law. Born in the former British Colony of Hong Kong in 1950, Wong came to the United States in the 1960s, working her way through college and law school as a waitress. She became one of the first non-U.S. citizens to be licensed to practice law in New York and Ohio and has since become a citizen. Over the last two decades, her firm has helped employers obtain work permits for executives and has assisted thousands of people in coming to the United State to become permanent residents, advance their educations, and pursue career opportunities. In addition to running a highly successful law firm, Wong is also a tireless civic leader, serving as the first Asian-American president of the Cleveland Chapter of the Federal Bar Association. The Ohio Supreme Court appointed her a charter member of the Continuing Legal Education Commission for attorneys, where she is currently serving as a member of its racial task force. In addition, Wong contributes her time and expertise to the boards of diverse organizations, including educational institutions such as Notre Dame College, Cuyahoga Community College and the Northeast Ohio Commission on Higher Education, among many other civic and professional organizations. In 1998 she received the highly coveted Ellis Island Medal of Honor for her outstanding achievements and contributions to the United States.

about the authors

John Sobczak has been a commercial photographer for more than 20 years. He has received numerous regional and national awards for his images and has worked for many of the Fortune 500 companies, including Ford Motor Company, Daimler-Chrysler, General Motors, AT&T and IBM, as well as such publications as *Newsweek, Fortune, Entrepreneur* and *Parade. Cleveland Classics* is his third book, a followup to *Motor City Memoirs* and *Wordlens*. Sobczak lives in Bloomfield Township, Michigan, with his wife, Jackie, and seven-year old-daughter, Alex.

Terry Troy has been a professional writer for more than 20 years and has written for a wide variety of publications, as well as radio and television. He previously worked with ABC/Capital Cities Fairchild Fashion Merchandising Group in Manhattan as a Senior Editor before moving on to ICD Publications on Long Island where he was a publisher with *HomeWorld Business*. A Cleveland native, Troy moved back to the Greater Cleveland area in 1998. He currently works as a freelance writer and journalist. His work has appeared in *The Plain Dealer, Northern Ohio Live, Cleveland Magazine* and *IndustryWeek*, among other national and local publications.

Richard Osborne, a writer and editor for more than 30 years, has been honored with dozens of regional and national journalism awards. Past president of The Press Club of Cleveland, he has been a newspaper and magazine editor, author and editor of regional books, and radio news director. He currently serves as editorial director of *Ohio Magazine* and president of The Osborne Group and ROP, Ltd., managing projects for numerous clients including *The Plain Dealer, The Columbus Dispatch* and *BusinessWeek.* He also writes a column for *The Morning Journal* in Lorain. Osborne and his wife, Della, live in Avon. They have four children and three grandchildren.

Jonathan Browning has been an award-winning graphic designer for more than 20 years. He has served as art director for such publications as *IW Growing Companies* in Ohio, *Millimeter Magazine* in New York and *Élan Magazine* in Southern California. Today he is the principal of Brown Ink Design + Gallery where he develops print collateral, annual reports, publications and special projects. He has developed work for such clients as AT&T, Intel, *BusinessWeek* and the Cleveland Cavaliers. In addition, Browning teaches design courses at Cuyahoga Community College and does fine art paintings that are sold locally. He currently lives and works in Downtown Cleveland.

The Harold H. Burton Main Avenue Bridge

acknowledgments

Creating a book filled with stories by so many different individuals requires a great deal of time and effort. Scheduling, securing, indeed simply finding some of the individuals involved countless hours and we never could have done it alone. To all who gave their time and energy in making this book a reality, we would like to say thank you.

Steve Oatley

Del Ready, Immortal Investments Publishing

Richard Gildenmeister, Cleveland's premier bookseller for half a century

Geri Pastor, Cleveland Browns

Michael Benz, CEO, United Way

Robert Tayek, Director of Media and Public Relations, Catholic Diocese of Cleveland

Angela Calman, Chief Communications Officer, Cleveland Clinic

Jim Blazar, Chief Marketing Officer, Cleveland Clinic

Dan Sobczak, Eric Smith, Allan Barnes, James Thomas, Photographic assistants

Ken McCahan, Event Manager, Gund Arena

Amanda Mercado, Cleveland Cavaliers

Eleanor Fanslau, Assistant to Sam Miller

Joe Corrigan, Comfort Inn

Nikki Scandalios & Julie A. Clark, The Cleveland Orchestra

Donna Brock, Director of External Affairs, Cleveland Museum of Art

Richard Baker, Messina, Baker Entertainment

Christina Papadopoulos, Baker Winoker Ryder

Alina Martinet, WKYC

Allison Brotherton

Bob Jermain, Make-up, Drew Carey

Brian Marek, Executive assistant, Margaret Wong Associates

Deborah McGee, Personal assistant to Ruby Dee

Barbara Wright, Klasky Csupo

Tim Mueller, Former Chief Strategic Officer for the City of Cleveland

Park Spencer, Rubenstein Associates, Inc.

Phyllis DeFranco, Secretary to Mr. Conway

Jill DeVincens, Personal assistant to Phil Donahue

Emil Jacobs, Assistant to Joe Eszterhas

Cathi Banks, Former assistant to Arsenio Hall

Julie Peres-Lanke, Assistant to Patty Heaton

Eileen Fallon, Secretary to Alex Machaskee

Debbie Warden, Executive assistant to the Chairman and CEO, Invacare

Cressida Suttles, Assistant to Al Roker

Alex Peltier, Tyler Baldridge, Matt George, Casey Roel, Kyle Leroux and Kevin Simonson,
Santa Fe Christian High School football team members with Brian Sipe

Jodie Capes, Former assistant to Molly Shannon

Susie Frazier Mueller

Traci Purdum Von Duyke

Susan M. Kornfield and Angela M. Sujek, Bodmann LLP

The Willow Avenue Bridge

cleveland classics

great stories from the north coast